Surrealist Poetry

Surrealist Poetry

An Anthology

Translated and edited by Willard Bohn

Bloomsbury Academic
An imprint of Bloomsbury Publishing Inc

B L O O M S B U R Y

NEW YORK • LONDON • OXFORD • NEW DELHI • SYDNEY

Bloomsbury Academic
An imprint of Bloomsbury Publishing Inc

1385 Broadway
New York
NY 10018
USA

50 Bedford Square
London
WC1B 3DP
UK

www.bloomsbury.com

BLOOMSBURY and the Diana logo are trademarks of Bloomsbury Publishing Plc

First published 2017

Library of Congress Cataloging-in-Publication Data
A catalog record for this book is available from the Library of Congress.

ISBN: HB: 978-1-4411-9977-5
PB: 978-1-4411-5314-2
ePub: 978-1-4411-7455-0
ePDF: 978-1-4411-1394-8

Cover design: Eleanor Rose
Cover image © Jersey Heritage Collections

Typeset by Fakenham Prepress Solutions, Fakenham, Norfolk NR21 8NN
Printed and bound in the United States of America

Contents

Introduction

At first glance, Surrealism would hardly seem to need much of an introduction. In view of its unprecedented global impact, as Anna Balakian has argued, it constitutes "the major poetic and artistic current of the twentieth century."[1] Of the dozens of movements that have vied for this honor since the turn of the century, Surrealism has proven to be the most influential and the most persistent. Although abstraction has enjoyed a huge success, for example, it has been limited almost entirely to art. Surrealism's most serious rival is (or was) probably Cubism, since it had an important impact on both literature and painting. Another leading contender is Expressionism, however one chooses to define it, which influenced a broad spectrum of aesthetic creations. Still, the fact remains that Surrealism is the only movement to span the greater part of the twentieth century and to enjoy widespread popularity. The man in the street, from Tokyo to Stockholm, cares little for modern aesthetics, but he has definitely heard of Surrealism. Quite possibly he has seen a mainstream film by Luis Buñuel, such as *Viridiana* or *The Discrete Charm of the Bourgeoisie*. Almost certainly he has been exposed to Salvador Dalí's melting watches and to the antics of the artist himself. Indeed, *The Persistence of Memory* is one of the more famous paintings of the twentieth century. With the possible exception of Grant Wood's *American Gothic*, it has been parodied more often than any other work in America.

Whereas Surrealist art and film have achieved widespread success, Surrealist poetry has languished in their shadow. While generation after generation of poets has absorbed Surrealism's lesson, while they have revitalized modern poetry in general, their efforts have received relatively little attention. At best their work is known to a small group of cognoscenti who are either practicing poets themselves or who take a scholarly interest in the subject. Since Surrealism was originally conceived as a literary movement, this is highly ironic to say the least. Founded by André Breton in 1924, it sought to examine the unconscious realm by means of the written and/or spoken word. In the first place, it attempted to expand the ability of language to evoke irrational states and improbable events. In the second place, it consistently strove to transcend the linguistic status quo. By stretching language to its limits and beyond, the Surrealists transformed it into an instrument for exploring the human psyche. Like the Dada movement, from which it gradually emerged, Surrealism aimed not only to redefine language but to reconceptualize its basic function. Henceforth, words were viewed as independent entities rather than static objects. "Les mots ... ont fini de jouer," Breton explained at one point; "les mots font l'amour" ("Words ... have finished playing silly games. Words have discovered how to make love").[2]

Since several misunderstandings have arisen concerning the Surrealist enterprise, it is helpful to review its basic tenets. Although these were not all adopted at the same moment nor endorsed with equal vigor by everyone, they were essentially six in number. As originally defined, Surrealism appeared to be governed by a single principle, which had led Breton and Soupault to compose *Les Champs magnétiques* (*Magnetic Fields*) as early as 1919. Reflecting the excitement that accompanied those original experiments, the *First Manifesto* emphasized the role of psychic automatism:

> SURREALISME, n.m. Automatisme psychique pur par lequel on se propose d'exprimer, soit verbalement, soit de toute autre

> manière, le fonctionnement réel de la pensée. Dictée de la pensée, en l'absence de tout contrôle exercé par la raison, en dehors de toute préoccupation morale ou esthétique.
>
> ENCYCL. *Philos.* Le surréalisme repose sur la croyance à la réalité supérieure de certaines formes d'associations négligées jusqu'à lui, à la toute-puissance du rêve, au jeu désintéressé de la pensée. Il tend à ruiner définitivement tous les autres mécanismes psychiques et a se substituer a eux dans la résolution des principaux problèmnes de la vie.
>
> (SURREALISM, n. Pure psychic automatism by which we propose to express--either verbally or in writing or in some other manner—the true functioning of thought. The dictation of thought, in the absence of all control exercised by reason, outside all aesthetic and moral preoccupations.
>
> ENCYCL. Philos. Surrealism rests on a belief in the superior reality of certain forms of association neglected until now, in the omnipotence of dream, in the disinterested play of thought. Ultimately it tends to destroy all other psychic mechanisms and to take their place in resolving the principal problems of life.)[3]

Despite these remarks, psychic automatism was destined to play a limited role in Surrealism. Most, if not all, Surrealists found it more rewarding to subject irrational impulses to some sort of conscious control. Breton himself distinguished between Surrealist texts, which were purely automatic, and Surrealist poems, where the products of unconscious activity were scrupulously ordered. Although it received less attention initially, a second principle that assumed a key role was *le merveilleux* ("*the marvelous*"). Varying from one period to the next, the marvelous was defined essentially as exacerbated beauty (*Oeuvres*, 319). Embodying anxiety associated with the human condition, it provoked a revelatory shudder in the reader or viewer. This explains Surrealism's preoccupation with eerie images and enigmatic adventures. An additional concept, again barely adumbrated initially, was *le hasard objectif* ("*objective chance*"). The Surrealists believed the most powerful imagery was that which caused the greatest surprise. The way to create marvelous images, Breton declared, was to combine two apparently unrelated terms that possessed hidden affinities (*Oeuvres*, 324). One of the methods for achieving this goal was via psychic automatism. Another relied on chance operations such as those employed in an exercise called *le cadavre exquis* ("*the exquisite cadaver*"), where several people each contributed a word to form a random sentence.

By the time the *Second Manifesto* appeared, six years later, two more principles had been added to the Surrealist program. One of these, which Breton called "the supreme point" (or alternatively "the sublime point"), sought to revive the medieval concept of *coincidentia oppositorum*. "Tout porte à croire," he announced, "qu'il existe un certain point de l'esprit d'où la vie et la mort, le réel et l'imaginaire, le passé et le futur, le communicable et l'incommunicable, le haut et le bas cessent d'être perçus contradictoirement" ("According to all indications, a certain point exists in the mind where life and death, the real and the imaginary, the past and the future, the communicable and the incommunicable, the high and the low cease to be perceived as contradictions") (*Oeuvres*, 781). One of Surrealism's tasks was thus to abolish traditional antitheses, which were considered to be completely arbitrary, including the distinction between beauty and ugliness, truth and falsehood, and good and evil (*Oeuvres*, 782).

Since Surrealism was a revolutionary movement devoted to radical change, the decision to espouse Marxism was another logical step. To attempt to liberate humanity without correcting widespread social abuse was felt to be elitist, irresponsible, and counter-productive. Freedom in the psychological domain could never be achieved without political and economic freedom and vice versa. Although Breton's efforts to join the French Communist Party were eventually rebuffed, like his colleagues he continued to subscribe to Marxist principles. The final concept to be incorporated into the Surrealist program was that of *l'amour fou* ("*delirious love*"). Although it was not formally adopted until 1937, when Breton published a book of the same name, its roots extended back a number of years. In particular, the *Second Manifesto* celebrated love as the "seule [idée] capable de reconcilier tout homme, momentanément ou non, avec l'idée de *vie*" ("only [idea] capable of reconciling every individual, momentarily or not, with the idea of *life*") (*Oeuvres*, 823). Like the other principles we have examined, total, passionate commitment was conceived as a liberating force.

As Breton and his colleagues insisted, Surrealism intended, above all, to improve the quality of life. While its accomplishments were largely aesthetic, it aimed to revolutionize the manner in which we view existence, both subjective and objective. With this end in mind, it offered solutions to a whole series of problematic relationships. One such problem was the relation between the individual and the unconscious, which had only recently been discovered. By devising methods to gain access to this secret domain, it gave new meaning to the ancient Greek maxim "Know thyself." At the same time, Surrealism strove to redefine the relation between each person and the physical world. Whereas the quest for the supreme point required one to re-conceive reality in terms of unity rather than difference, the doctrines of objective chance and the marvelous called attention to its exceptional beauty. In addition, as we have seen, the Surrealists were determined to alter the relation between the individual and society, as well as that between man and woman. Consistent with Surrealism's eclectic origins, they experienced no difficulty in combining Freud with the alchemist Fulcanelli, and

Eros with Marx. Their goal was to transform the process of seeing, thinking, and feeling in order to arrive at complete liberation. Ultimately, Surrealism attempted to effect a total revolution in the way we perceive the universe and ourselves.

As noted previously, Surrealist artists and filmmakers have received much more attention than their literary colleagues. One of the reasons for this discrepancy has to do with the medium of expression they have chosen to employ. Unlike printed texts, paintings and films offer the illusion of being immediately accessible. Although viewers may have no idea what they really mean, the visual images impinge upon their retinas without need of mediation. The fact that many of the images appear to be realistic, that many objects can actually be identified, reenforces the viewer's impression. By contrast, the average reader needs all the energy he or she can muster to decipher many Surrealist poems. While the paintings and films contain numerous playful elements, the poetry requires a lot of hard work. Like *The Persistence of Memory*, *The Discrete Charm of the Bourgeoisie* is enormously entertaining. Although many Surrealist poems turn out to be equally charming, to the uninitiated they may merely seem frustrating.

Another reason Surrealist poetry has fared less well than its visual counterparts is again related to its medium of expression. Poetry is compelled to express itself not only in language, but in a specific language, which limits its audience still further. Until fairly recently, however, few Surrealist poets had been translated into other tongues. Even now, anyone wishing to read an author's complete works must often consult a foreign edition. The scarcity of multi-language translations into English is equally problematic. While selections exist of the work of some of the individuals included in this volume, readers seeking to compare French and Spanish poets have faced two awkward choices. They could either acquire numerous books translated into English, or they could attempt to read the texts in the language in which they were originally written. Ironically, although these latter readers have an undeniable advantage, a serious problem remains. The few bilingual anthologies published in the past focus on a single source language. This unfortunate circumstance reflects the situation in academia in general, where few scholars are equipped to study Surrealist texts written in multiple languages.

To the best of my knowledge, this is the first bilingual anthology to acknowledge Surrealism's linguistic diversity. Since it features translations from only two languages (plus a brief excursion into Catalan), it is a modest attempt, but one that at least points in the right direction. Unlike my earlier volume, *The Dada Market* (1993), which provides a broader sample, it concentrates on poets who reside in French- and Spanish-speaking countries. While I was tempted to adopt a similar approach in this book, I was finally dissuaded by the sheer bulk of the material available. Although Dada has enjoyed considerable success over the years, Surrealism has been much more popular. Instead of translating one or two texts by a great many poets, I have chosen a smaller number of authors so as to include a larger selection of their works. In every case, enough material has been included to permit the reader to form an accurate idea of the poet's style and subject matter. Although the more important authors receive more attention, as is only just, their lesser known colleagues are far from neglected. Despite the fact that the anthology is basically restricted to two languages, the reader will find it is surprisingly diverse. The twenty-three writers chosen for comparison are not limited to just France and Spain, but also come from Belgium, Egypt, Martinique, Mauritius, Mexico, Chile, and Peru.

Since Surrealism was invented in Paris, the importance of French comes as no surprise. That Spanish and Catalan were destined to be such fertile proving grounds resulted from a combination of historical circumstances and personal taste. By the time the poets residing in Spain were exposed to Surrealism, they had exhausted the possibilities of Ultraism and Creationism and were seeking a new source of inspiration. Like their colleagues in Catalonia, many members of the Generation of '27 embraced the Surrealist movement with open arms. Some of the Spanish writers spent long periods in France, where they learned about Surrealism firsthand. Like Salvador Dalí, Luís Buñuel, and Joan Miró, one or two even settled in Paris permanently. And since Surrealism was an evangelical movement, several French poets traveled to Spain in order to spread the latest word. André Breton lectured in Barcelona in 1922, for example, and Louis Aragon spoke at the Residencia de Estudiantes in Madrid in 1925.[4] Most of the Latin American poets, at least initially, learned about Surrealism either in Madrid or in Paris (or both). Like their literary forebearers, many of them were attached to diplomatic missions that allowed them to spend long periods of time abroad. In turn, they served as important conduits between the Old World and the New, introducing Surrealism to their friends at home.

Perhaps the greatest tribute to Surrealism's enduring value is that three of the poets included in this anthology were eventually awarded the Nobel Prize (Vicente Aleixandre, Pablo Neruda, and Octavio Paz). Ironically, for reasons that are difficult to grasp, no Surrealist poet writing in French has ever received this honor. Perhaps the original impulse was simply too intense, too chaotic, to receive official recognition. Perhaps it needed to be refined by a foreign intelligence and shaped in an epic mold. Or again, perhaps the revolutionary fervor of the original enterprise succeeeded in alienating the literary establishment outside France, as well as within (as, indeed, it was meant to). At this point, I can only leave these questions to the reader to decide. However, one explains this state of affairs, one thing seems abundantly clear: Surrealism has cast a long, indelible shadow from the birth of the movement up to the present day. Or rather, as one of my readers suggested, it has functioned as a powerful beacon, attracting poets and painters from all over the globe like moths to a creative flame. On the one hand, Surrealism has led to the creation of a vast body of exciting, innovative works. On the other, as the adjective "surrealistic" testifies, it has affected the way in which we view ourselves and the world around us.

Readers who are already familiar with the Surrealist movement may be surprised at some of the principles that have guided the selection and organization of the following texts. Scholars, in particular, will no doubt regret the absence of a critical apparatus, historical observations, and an extensive bibliography. However, since the anthology was conceived as a joyful experience, rather than as a scholarly presentation, I have adopted a more streamlined approach. Above all, I would like the reader to approach the poems in the spirit in which they were originally written for the sheer pleasure of it. Readers, who want to learn more about the Surrealist experiments with language, will find a brief bibliography at the end. Possessing few critical or historical pretensions, this anthology is intended primarily as an introduction to Surrealist poetry. Toward this end, I have chosen examples of the most important kinds of poems from individuals writing in a variety of traditions. Although the anthology does not attempt to provide complete coverage, it singles out the more important members of the various groups.

Following in the footsteps of the Dada movement, Surrealism was the second movement to emerge during the twentieth century that was truly international in scope. Notwithstanding this fact, literary histories inevitably divide the Surrealists into groups according to their geographical location and analyse their accomplishments accordingly. In order to avoid categorizing the poets included in this anthology by their country of origin, therefore, I have decided to list them in alphabetical order. Had they been organized according to the geographical model, Paris, Madrid, and Barcelona would have dwarfed the other centers by comparison. Thus, I have sought to stress the movement's international character by playing down the poets' national origins. It is not a question of promoting some centers as equally important to others, but rather simply of giving them all equal exposure. Indeed, by removing each poet from his or her particular group, I am forcing each one to justify his or her poetry independently. Each poem must stand or fall according to its own merits and by comparison with the other poems in the book. Arranging the texts alphabetically by author seems to be a good way to avoid any sort of bias. I would like readers to decide for themselves whether an individual poet is any good or not. I also hope they will consider what the various writers have in common despite the national and linguistic differences that separate them.

As one might expect, the level of accomplishment varies from one poet to the next and even from poem to poem. It should come as no surprise that the Surrealists were not uniformly brilliant and that they were capable of writing poetry that was less than perfect. As the reader will discover, some of the poets were truly revolutionary, and others were less extreme in their desire to break with tradition. Some of the poems constitute a radical critique of poetic language and form, while others attempt less ambitious reforms. More than anything, I have included works that I think are interesting, which will appeal to the reader on one or more levels. I also hope that readers who possess the requisite language skills will attempt to decipher the original poems and compare them with my own versions. However, the real subject of *Surrealist Poetry* is not translation, but poetry. More precisely, the volume is concerned with exploring the possibilities of the poetic act and its psychological, social, and aesthetic ramifications. The real heroes of this book are the Surrealists themselves, who included some amazingly creative people.

Notes

1 Anna Balakian, "Surrealism," in *The New Princeton Encyclopedia of Poetry and Poetics*, ed. Alex Preminger et al. (Princeton: Princeton University Press, 1993), 1236–7.

2 André Breton, *Position politique du surréalisme* (1935) (Paris: Denoël-Gonthier, 1972), 115.

3 André Breton, *Manifeste du surréalisme* in *Oeuvres complètes*, ed. Marguerite Bonnet et al. (Paris: Gallimard, 1988), vol. I, 328. Cited in the text, hereafter, as *Oeuvres*.

4 C. B. Morris reproduces the texts of five different lectures in *Surrealism and Spain, 1920–1936* (Cambridge: Cambridge University Press, 1972), 214–39.

Rafael Alberti

Born in Puerto de Santa María, Spain, Rafael Alberti (1902–99) arrived in Madrid in 1917, where he devoted himself to painting, as well as to poetry. In 1925, he was awarded the Premio Nacional de Literatura for his first book of poetry, *Marinero en tierra* (*Landlocked Sailor*). His best-known poem collections followed soon after: *Cal y Canto* (*Passion and Form*), in 1927, and *Sobre los ángeles* (*Concerning the Angels*), in 1928. The editor of several journals, Alberti was closely associated with avant-garde artists and writers, such as Federico García Lorca, Juan Gris, Salvador Dalí, Luis Buñuel, and Vicente Aleixandre. During the Spanish Civil War (1936–9), he served as secretary of the Alliance of Anti-Fascist Intellectuals, but was forced to flee Spain in 1939. Thereafter, he lived in Mexico, Argentina, and Italy, where he continued to write and to paint. Following General Franco's death in 1975, Alberti was finally able to return to his native land.

Engaño

Alguien detrás, a tu espalda,
tapándote los ojos con palabras.

Detrás de ti, sin cuerpo,
sin alma.

Ahumada voz de sueño cortado.
Ahumada voz cortada.

Con palabras, vidrios falsos.

Ciega, por un túnel de oro,
de espejos malos,
con la muerte
darás en un subterráneo.

Tú allí sola, con la muerte,
en un subterráneo.

Y alguien detrás, a tu espalda,
siempre.

El Ángel Del Misterio

Un sueño sin faroles y una humedad de olvidos,
pisados por un nombre y una sombra.
No sé si por un nombre o muchos nombres,
si por una sombra o muchas sombras.
Reveládmelo.

Deceit

Some one behind you, just in back of you,
covering your eyes with words.

Behind you, with neither body
nor soul.

The smoky voice of a dream
cut short.

With words, false window panes.

Blindly, through a tunnel of gold
lined with evil mirrors,
you will join death
far underground.

You, all alone with death,
far underground.

And someone behind you, just in back of you,
always.

The Angel of Mystery

A shadowy dream and a forgetful moisture,
trampled by a name and a shadow.
I don't know if by one name or many names,
if by one shadow or many shadows.
Reveal its meaning to me.

Sé que habitan los pozos frías voces,
que son de un solo cuerpo o muchos cuerpos,
de una alma sola o muchas almas.
No sé.
Decídmelo.

Que un caballo sin nadie va estampando
a su amazona antigua por los muros.
Que en las almenas grita, muerto, alguien
que yo toqué, dormido, en un espejo,
que yo, mudo, le dije …
No sé.
Explicádmelo.

El Ángel Falso

Para que yo anduviera entre los nudos de las raíces
y las viviendas óseas de los gusanos.
Para que yo escuchara los crujidos descompuestos del mundo
y mordiera la luz petrificada de los astros,
al oeste de mi sueño levantaste tu tienda, ángel falso.

Los que unidos por una misma corriente de agua me veis,
los que atados por una traición y la caída de una estrella me
    escucháis,
acogeos a las voces abandonadas de las ruinas.
Oíd la lentitud de una piedra que se dobla hacia la muerte.

No os soltéis de las manos.

Hay arañas que agonizan sin nido
y yedras que al contacto de un hombro se incendian y llueven
    sangre.

I know that frigid voices inhabit wells,
that they have one body or many bodies,
a single soul or many souls.
I don't know.
Decide for me.

That a wild horse is stamping its former rider's
image on the city walls.
That a dead man screams on the battlements,
someone I touched,
asleep, in a mirror …
I don't know.
Explain it to me.

The False Angel

So I might pass between the roots' knots
and the worms' osseous dwellings.
So I might hear the world's decayed creaking
and bite the petrified starlight,
false angel, you have raised your tent to the west of my dreams.

You who united by a common stream regard me,
you who combined by a betrayal and a falling star listen
to me,
welcome the abandoned voices of the ruins.
Hear how slowly each stone turns toward death.

Do not loosen your hands.

Spiders are dying far from their webs,
and ivy catches fire and rains blood at the touch of a
shoulder.

La luna transparenta el esqueleto de los largatos.
Si os acordáis del cielo,
la cólera del frío se erguirá aguda en los cardos
o en el disimulo de las zanjas que estrangulan
el único descanso de las auroras: las aves.
Quienes piensen en los vivos verán moldes de arcilla
habitados por ángeles infieles, infatigables:
los ángeles sonámbulos que gradúan las órbitas de la fatiga.

¿Para qué seguir andando?
Las humedades son íntimas de los vidrios en punta
y después de un mal sueño la escarcha despierta clavos
o tijeras capaces de helar el luto de los cuervos.

Todo ha terminado.
Puedes envanecerte, en la cauda marchita de los cometas que se
hunden,
de que mataste a un muerto,
de que diste a una sombra la longitud desvelada del llanto,
de que asfixiaste el estertor de las capas atmosféricas.

Sin Más Remedio

Tenía yo que salir de la tierra,
la tierra tenía que escupirme de una vez para siempre como un
hijo bastardo,
como un hijo temido a quien no esperan nunca reconocer las
ciudades.
Había que llorar hasta mover los trenes y trastornar a gritos las
horas de las marcas,
dando al cielo motivo para abandonarse a una pena sin lluvia.
Había que expatriarse involuntariamente,
dejar ciertas alcobas,
ciertos ecos,
ciertos ojos vacíos.

The moon shines through the lizards' bones.
If you recall the sky,
the angry cold will rise sharply among the thistles
or in the hidden ravines that strangle
the dawn's sole source of peace: birds.
Whoever considers the living will find clay molds
inhabited by disloyal, untiring angels:
sonambulist angels who regulate the spheres of fatigue.

Why continue?
The dampness embraces the pointed window panes,
and emerging from a nightmare the frost awakens nails
or scissors capable of freezing the crows' grief.

It's all over.
You can pride yourself in the withered train of sinking
comets,
that you murdered a dead man,
that you revealed the tears' watchful longitude to a shadow,
that you stiffled the atmospheric strata's death rattle.

Without Further Ado

I had to leave the earth,
the earth had to spit me out once and for all like a
bastard son,
like a fearful son cities hope to avoid recognizing.
We had to cry until the trains moved and shout until the tides'
timetables were disrupted,
lending the sky a reason to express its rainless grief.
We had to emigrate involuntarily,
to leave certain bedrooms,
certain echoes,
certain vacant eyes.

Ya voy.

Tenias tú que vivir más de una media vida sin conocer las voces que ya llegan
pasadas por el mundo,
más aislado que el frío de una torre encargada de iluminar el rumbo de las
aves perdidas,
sobre el mar que te influye hasta hacerte saladas las palabras.
Tú tenías a la fuerza que haber nacido solo y sufrido sin gloria para decirme:

Hace ya treinta años que ni leo los periódicos: mañana hará buen tiempo.

Espantapájaros

Ya en mi alma pesaban de tal modo los muertos futuros
que no podía andar ni un solo paso sin que las piedras revelaran sus entrañas.
¿Qué gritan y defienden esos trajes retorcidos por las exhalaciones?
Sangran ojos de mulos cruzados de escalofríos.
Se hace imposible el cielo enre tantas tumbas anegadas de setas corrompidas.

¿Adónde ir con las ansias de los que han de morirse?
La noche se desploma por un exceso de equipaje secreto.
Alabad a la chispa que electrocuta las huestes y los rebaños.
Un hombre y una vaca perdidos.

¿Qué nuevas desventuras esperan a las hojas para este otoño?
Mi alma no puede ya con tanto cargamento sin destino.

I'm going now.

You had to live more than half your life without the faded voices
that are now heard everywhere,
more isolated than a towering cold charged with illuminating the path of lost birds,
overlooking the influential sea that renders even your words salty.
Of necessity you had to have been born alone and suffered ingloriously to tell me:

I haven't read a newspaper in thirty years: tomorrow we will have good weather.

Scarecrow

My soul was so oppressed by future deaths that the stones spilled their guts at every step.
Those clothes twisted by the vapors, what are they shouting and pleading?
Bleeding mules' eyes traversed by shudders.
The sky is becoming impossible between so many tombs drowned in rotten mushrooms.

Where can those who are destined to die turn in their anguish?
Night collapses under the excess weight of secret baggage.
Hooray for the spark that electrocutes the hosts and the herds.
A man and a cow lost.

What new misfortunes await the leaves this fall?
My soul cannot cope with so much floating cargo.

El sueño para preservarse de las lluvias intenta una alquería.
Anteanoche no aullaron ya las lobas.

¿Qué espero rodeado de muertos al filo de una madrugada
indecisa?

Sermón De La Sangre

Me llama, me grita, me advierte, me despeña y me alza, hace
de mi cabeza un yunque en medio de las olas, un despiadado
yunque contra quien deshacerse zumbando.

Háy que tomar el tren, le ure, No lo hay. Salió. Y ahora me
dice que ella misma lo hizo volar al alba, desaparecer
íntegro ante un amanecer de toros desangrándose a la boca,
de un túnel,

Sé que estoy en la edad de obedecerla, de ir detrás de su voz
que atraviesa desde la hoja helada de los trigos hasta el
pico del ave que nunca pudo tomar tierra y aguarda que los
cielos se hagan cuarzo algún día para al fin detenerse un
solo instante.

La edad terrible de violentar con ella las puertas más cerradas,
los años más hundidos por los que hay que descender a
tientas, siempre con el temor de perder una mano o de quedar
sujero or un pie a la última rendija, esa que filtra un gas
que deja ciego y hace oir la caída del agua en otro mundo,
la edad terrible está presente, ha llegado con ella, y la sirvo:
mientras me humilla, me levanta, me inunda, me desquicia,
me seca, me abandona, me hace correr de nuevo, y yo no sé
llamarla de otro modo:

Mi sangre.

To protect itself from the rains dream initiates a hamlet.
The wolves did not howl the night before last.

Surrounded by death on the edge of an uncertain dawn, what am
I waiting for?

Blood Sermon

It calls me, screams at me, warns me, hurls me through the air,
transforms my head into an anvil surrounded by waves, a
pitiless anvil humming with destruction.

Get on board, I urge you. But the train has already departed.
They tell me my blood sent it flying toward the dawn,
where it will disappear completely, toward a dawn of bulls
bleeding to death at the mouth of a tunnel.

I know my age compels me to obey my blood, to penetrate its voice
which transfixes everything from the wheat stalk's icy leaf
to the beak of the bird who can never land and who awaits
the day when the sky will turn to quartz, so it can finally
stop for a moment.

I am the terrible age to break the heaviest doors with my blood,
the years most squandered by those who descend groping in
the dark, fearing to lose a hand or to catch a foot in the ultimate
crevice, from which a blinding gas issues with the sound of
water falling in another world. The terrible age is upon me, has
arrived with my blood, and I long to serve it: while it humiliates
me, elevates me, inundates me, unhinges me, drains me,
abandons me, makes me flee again, and I don't know how else to
call it:

My blood.

Dos Niños

Ya tú nada más esperas la aparición de esos resortes ocultos que se abren
a los delgados pasillos donde la luz se desalienta al presentir la muerte.

¿No se asustará el cielo de lo prematuro de tu viaje?
Te lo pregunta un alma que todavía le importa un poco la tierra.

Esos delgados pasillos que desembocan al invierno de un patio,
¿no congelan el ansia de eternidad que silba por tu sangre?
El tragaluz que se angustia sin vidrio para absorber la pena de una nube,
¿paraliza en tus párpados el deseo de las horas sin orillas?
Es pronto,
demasiado pronto para que un niño se abandone a las sombras.

Bien se ve que la noche le considera un muchacho distinto
del que en el día se ahoga en una gota de agua.
¿Qué sabe la golondrina del insomnio del buho?

Por caridad,
matadle sin que la aurora lo adivine.

Ha dejado su cabeza olvidada entre dos alambres.
Ha gritado su corazón para que los ecos se le volvieran en contra.
Preguntad por sus manos a las agujas que se pierden en los lechos.

¿Adónde va ese niño que equivoca las esquinas?

Two Boys

No longer do you await the apparition of those occult springs that open
onto slender corridors where light loses heart at the intimation of death.

Won't the sky be frightened by your premature journey?
This question is posed by a soul – still clinging to the earth.

Those slender corridors ending in a winter's courtyard, don't they freeeze the
anxiety of eternity whistling through your blood?
The anxious skylight lacking glass to absorb a cloud's grief,
doesn't it paralyze the desire of boundless hours in your eyelids?
It is soon,
too soon for a boy to abandon the shadows.

One easily perceives that the night differentiates between this boy and the one
who drowns in a drop of water during the day.
What does the swallow know of the owl's insomnia?

For pity's sake,
do away with him without the dawn finding out.

He has forgotten his head between two wires.
His heart has shouted for the echoes to turn against him.
Question with gestures the needles that disappear in the beds.

Where is that boy going who confuses the corners?

Fragmentos De Un Deseo

… Aquí, cuando el aire traiciona la rectitud de los lirios, es condenado
a muerte por un remolino de agua.
No es sombra de amargura la que adelantan los árboles hacia el ocaso.
Te informará de esto el guardabosque que costean los fríos.

Si en tu país una ilusión se pierde a lo largo de los calores, en el mío las
nieves te ayudarán a encontrarla.
Si la huella de un zapato no dispone de tiempo para dormir a una violeta,
aquí entretiene su vida en recoger el ciclo de las lluvias.

Es triste,
muy triste saber que una mano estampada en el polvo dura menos que el
recorrido que abre una hoja al morirse.

¿No te apenan esos hilos que desfallecen de pronto contra tus mejillas
cuando despobladas de nubes se hielan en los estanques?

Fragments of a Desire

... Here, when the air betrays the lilies' rectitude, it is
condemned
to death by a whirlpool.
It is not a shadow of bitterness cast by the trees toward the
sunset.
The forest ranger whom the cold pays will tell you this.

If – an illusion in your land disappears during the heat, the snow
in mine will help you find it.
If a shoe's footprint lacks time to put a violet to
sleep,
it passes its time here reaping the cycle of the rains.

It is sad,
very sad to know that a hand stamped in the dust lasts less time
than
the path a leaf opens when it dies.

Don't you mourn for those threads that suddenly die against your
cheeks
when, deprived of clouds, they freeze in the ponds?

Vicente Aleixandre

Born in Seville, Spain, but raised in Málaga, Vicente Aleixandre (1898–1984) arrived in Madrid in 1909; he remained there for the rest of his life. Although trained as a lawyer, he devoted himself entirely to poetry from an early age due to ill health. His best-known poem collections are: *Espadas como labios* (*Swords like Lips*) (1932), *Pasión de la tierra* (*Passion of the Earth*) (1935), and *La destrucción o el amor* (*Destruction or Love*) (1932–3), for which he received the Premio Nacional de Literatura in 1933. During this period, Aleixandre began to associate with Pedro Salinas, Federico García Lorca, Jorge Guillén, and other poets based in Madrid, known collectively as the "Generation of 1927." Always in poor health, he remained in Madrid during the Spanish Civil War, but maintained his political independence. For this reason, Aleixandre's works were banned from 1936 to 1944 by the Franco regime. However, his brilliant poetic career continued unabated, and, in 1977, he received the Nobel Prize in Literature.

Vida

Esa sombra o tristeza masticada que pasa doliendo no oculta
las palabras, por más que los ojos no miren lastimados.

Doledme

No puedo perdonarte, no, por más que un lento vals levante esas olas de polvo fino, esos puntos dorados que son propiamente una invitación al sueño de la cabellera, a ese abandono largo que flamea luego débilmente ante el aliento de las lenguas cansadas

Pero el mar está lejos

Me acuerdo que un día una sirena verde del color de la Luna sacó su pecho herido, partido en dos como la boca, y me quiso besar sobre la sombra muerta, sobre las aguas quietas seguidoras. Le faltaba otro seno. No volaban abismos. No. Una rosa sentida, un pétalo de carne, colgaba de su cuello y se ahogaba en el agua morada, mientras la frente arriba, ensombrecida de alas palpitantes, se cargaba de sueño, de muerte joven, de esperanza sin hierba, bajo el aire sin aire. Los ojos no morían. Yo podría haberlos tenido en esta mano, acaso para besarlos, acaso para sorberlos, mientras reía precisamente por el hombro, contemplando una esquina de duelo, un pez brutal que derribaba el cantil contra su lomo.

Esos ojos de frío no me mojan la espera de tu llama, de las escamas pálidas de ansia. Aguárdame. Eres la virgen ola de ti misma, la materia sin tino que alienta entre lo negro, buscando el hormigueo que no grite cuando le hayan hurtado su secreto, sus sangrientas entrañas que salpiquen, (Ah, la voz: "Te quedarás ciego".) Esa carne en lingotes flagela la castidad valiente y secciona

Life

That shadow or masticated sorrow passing painfully by does not obscure words, however much one's eyes fail to express sorrow.

Hurt me.

I cannot forgive you, no, however much a slow waltz raises those waves of fine dust, those gilded motes that represent an invitation to the hair's dream, to that long abandon weakly blazing later before the exhausted tongues' breath.

But the sea is far away.

I remember that one day a green siren the color of the Moon pulled out her wounded breast, split in two like her mouth, and tried to kiss me on the dead shadow, on the still, devoted waters. Her other breast was missing. Abysses were not blown away. No. A tender rose, a petal of flesh, hung from her neck and was drowning in the violet water, while with her head up, overshadowed by palpitating wings, she filled herself with dream, with youthful death, with grassless hope, beneath the airless air. Her eyes were not dying. I could have held them in my hand and kissed them or sucked them, while she laughed over her shoulder, contemplating a dueling corner, a brutal fish demolishing the cliff against its spine.

Those eyes of cold do not dampen my hope of your flame, of the pallid scales of anguish. Wait for me. You are the virgin wave of yourself, senseless matter glowing in the dark, seeking the anthill that doesn't scream when they steal its secret, its bloody bowels that splatter. (Ah, the voice: "You will remain blind") That flesh in ingots whips the valiant chastity and divides the head into sections,

la frente despejando la idea, permitiendo a tres pájaros su aparición o su forma, su desencanto ante el cielo rendido.

¿Nada más?

Yo no soy ese tibio decapitado que pregunta la hora, en el segundo entre dos oleadas. No soy el desnivel suavísimo por el que rueda el aire encerrado, esperando su pozo, donde morir sobre una rosa sepultada. No soy el color rojo, ni el rosa, ni el amarillo que nace lentamente, hasta gritar de pronto notando la falta de destino, la meta de clamores confusos.

Más bien soy el columpio redivivo que matasteis anteayer.

Soy lo que soy. Mi nombre escondido.

El Silencio

Esa luz amarilla que la luna me envía es una historia larga que me acongoja más que un brazo desnudo. ¿Por qué me tocas, si sabes que no puedo responderte? ¿Por qué insistes nuevamente, si sabes que contra tu azul profundo, casi líquido, no puedo más que cerrar los ojos, ignorar las aguas muertas, no oír las músicas sordas de los peces de arriba, olvidar la forma de su cuadrado estanque? ¿Por qué abres tu boca reciente, para que yo sienta sobre mi cabeza que la noche no ama más que mi esperanza, porque espera verla convertida en deseo? ¿Por qué el negror de los brazos quiere tocarme el pecho y me pregunta por la nota de mi bella caja escondida, por esa cristalina palidez que se sucede siempre cuando un piano se ahoga, o cuando se escucha la extinguida nota del beso? Algo que es como un arpa que se hunde.

clarifying the idea, permitting the appearance or the shape of three birds, their disenchantment before the submissive sky.

Nothing else?

I am not that tepid, headless man who asks the time. In the second separating two waves I am not the gentle slope down which the enclosed air rolls, hoping for a well in which to die upon a buried rose. I am not the color red, nor the rose, nor yellow that is born slowly, until it soon screams noting the absence of destiny, the goal of confused cries.

Rather I am the resuscitated swing that you murdered the day before yesterday.

I am what I am. My name hidden.

Silence

The yellow light the moon sends me is a long story that distresses me more than a naked arm. Why do you touch me, knowing I can't respond? Why do you insist, knowing that against your dark, nearly liquid blue I can only close my eyes, ignore the dead waters, drown out the muffled music of the fish swimming above, forget the shape of their square pond? Why do you open your recent mouth so my head feels the night loves only my hope, because it hopes to see it transformed into desire? Why does your arms' darkness long to touch my chest and to demand the note hidden in my lovely box, for the crystalline pallor that succeeds itself whenever a piano drowns, or when a kiss' extinguished note rings out? Something like a sinking harp.

Pero tú, hermosísima, no quieres conocer este azul frío de que estoy revestido y besas la helada contracción de mi esfuerzo. Estoy quieto como el arco tirante, y todo para ignorarte, oh noche de los espaciós cardinales, de los torrentes de silencio y de lava. ¡Si tú vieras qué esfuerzo me cuesta guardar el equilibrio contra la opresión de tu seno, contra ese martillo de hierro que me está golpeando aquí, en el séptimo espacio intercostal, preguntándome por el contacto de dos epidermis! Lo ignoro todo. No quiero saber si el color rojo es antes o es después, si Dios lo sacó de su frente o si nació del pecho del primer hombre herido. No quiero saber si los labios son una larga línea blanca.

De nada me servirá ignorar la hora que es, no tener noción de la lucha cruel, de la aurora que me está naciendo entre mi sangre. Acabaré pronunciando unas palabras relucientes. Acabaré destellando entre los dientes tu muerte prometida, tu marmórea memoria, tu torso derribado, mientras me elevo con mi sueño hasta el amanecer radiante, hasta la certidumbre germinante que me cosquillea en los ojos, entre los párpados, prometiéndos a todos un mundo iluminado en cuanto yo me despierte.

Te beso, oh, pretérita, mientras miro el río en que te vas copiando, por último, el color azul de mi frente.

Palabras

Pero no importa que todo esté tranquilo.
(La palabra, esa lana marchita.)
Flor tú, muchacha casi desnuda, viva, viva
(la palabra, esa arena machacada).
Muchacha, con tu sombra qué dulce lucha

But you, exquisite beauty, you refuse to acknowledge this cold blue I am wearing, and you kiss my strength's frozen contraction. I am as quiet as a taut bow, just in order to ignore you, oh night of cardinal spaces, of torrents of silence and lava. If you could see how much strength I need to keep my balance against your breast's pressure, against that steel hammer pounding me here, in the seventh intercostal space, demanding the contact of two skins! I ignore everything. I don't want to know if the color red comes before or after, if God extracted it from his forehead or if it was born from the chest of the first man to be wounded. I don't want to know if your lips are a long white line.

I gain nothing by ignoring the time, by having no notion of the cruel struggle, of the dawn arising from my blood. I'll finally utter a few glittering words. I'll finally hold your promised death, your marble memory, your demolished torso, twinklng between my teeth, while I rise with my dream toward the radiant dawn, toward the sprouting certainty tickling my eyes, between my eyelids, promising everyone an illuminated world as soon as I awake.

I kiss you, oh past tense, while regarding the river in which you finish copying the blue color of my brow.

Words

But it doesn't matter if everything is calm.
(A word, so much faded yarn.)
Live, live young lady, nearly naked flower
(a word, so much powdered sand).
Young lady, with your shadow struggling gently

como una miel fugaz que casi muestra bordes.
(La palabra, la palabra, la palabra, qué torpe vientre
hinchado.)
Muchacha, te has manchado de espuma delicada.

Papel. Lengua de luto. Amenaza. Pudridero.
Palabras, palabras, palabras, palabras.
Iracundia. Bestial. Torpeza. Amarillez.
Palabras contra el vientre o muslos sucias.

No me esperes, ladina nave débil,
débil rostro ladeado que repasas
sobre un mar de nácar sostenido por manos.
Nave, papel o luto, borde o vientre,
palabra que se pierde como arena.

Las Águilas

El mundo encierra la verdad de la vida,
aunque la sangre mienta melancólicamente
cuando como mar sereno en la tarde
siente arriba el batir de las águilas libres.

Las plumas de metal,
las garras poderosas,
ese afán del amor o la muerte,
ese deseo de beber en los ojos con un pico de hierro,
de poder al fin besar lo exterior de la tierra,
vuela como el deseo,
como las nubes que a nada se oponen,
como el azul radiante, corazón ya de afuera
en que la libertad se ha abierto para el mundo.

like fleeting honey hinting at its edges.
(A word, a word, a word, what a clumsy swollen
belly.)
Young lady, you have soiled yourself with delicate foam.

Paper. Tongue of mourning. Menace. City dump.
Words, words, words, words.
Anger. Bestial. Clumsiness. Sallowness.
Words hanging filthy against the belly or thighs.

Don't wait for me, weak, crafty ship,
weak tilted face returning
on a lustrous, hand-held sea.
Ship, paper or mourning, edge or belly,
word that vanishes like sand.

The Eagles

The earth encloses the truth about life,
even though the blood tells melancholy lies
when, like the calm afternoon sea,
it senses the eagles flying freely overhead.

Their metal feathers,
their powerful claws,
their zeal for love or death
eager to drink from eyes with their iron beaks,
to kiss the world's outer edge at last
takes wing like desire,
like clouds that stand in the way of nothing,
like radiant blue, a heart already outside
where freedom displays itself to the world.

Las águilas serenas
no serán nunca esquifes,
no serán sueño o pájaro,
no serán caja donde olvidar lo triste,
donde tener guardado esmeraldas u ópalos.

El sol que cuaja en las pupilas,
que a las pupilas mira libremente,
es ave inmarcesible, vencedor de los pechos
donde hundir su furor contra un cuerpo amarrado.

Las violentas alas
que azotan rostros como eclipses,
que parten venas de zafiro muerto,
que seccionan la sangre coagulada,
rompen el viento en mil pedazos,
mármol o espacio impenetable
donde una mano muerta detenida
es el claror que en la noche fulgura.

Águilas como abismos,
como montes altísimos,
derriban majestades, troncos polvorientos,
esa verde hiedra que en los muslos
finge la lengua vegetal casi viva.

Se aproxima el momento en que la dicha consista
en desvestir de piel a los cuerpos humanos,
en que el celeste ojo victorioso
vea solo a la tierra como sangre que gira.

Águilas de metal sonorísimo,
arpas furiosas con su voz casi humana,
cantan la ira de amar los corazones,
amarlos con las garras estrujando su muerte.

The serene eagles
will never become skiffs,
nor a dream nor a bird,
nor a box in which to leave one's sorrow,
in which to keep emeralds or opals.

The sun congealing in the pupils,
gazing freely at the pupils,
is a lively bird, the conqueror of hearts
in which to sink its fury against a bound body.

The violent wings
beating against faces like eclipses,
splitting veins of dead sapphire,
dividing the coagulated blood,
break the wind into a thousand pieces,
marble or impenetrable space
where a dead hand held up
is the splendor that flashes in the night.

Eagles like chasms,
like the highest mountains,
overflow majestic things, dusty tree trunks,
green ivy gliding along one's thighs
pretending to be a vegetable tongue, nearly alive.

The moment is drawing near when happiness will consist
of stripping the skin from human bodies,
when the victorious celestial eye
will see the earth as a whirlpool of blood.

Eagles of the most resonant metal,
furious harps with nearly human voices,
sing the anger of falling in love with hearts,
of loving them and strangling them with their claws.

Las Manos

Mira tu mano, que despacio se mueve,
transparente, tangible, atravesada por la luz,
hermosa, viva, casi humana en la noche.
Con reflejo de luna, con dolor de mejilla, con vaguedad de
sueño mírala así crecer, mientras alzas el brazo,
búsqueda inútil de una noche perdida,
ala de luz que cruzando en silencio
toca carnal esa bóveda oscura.

No fosforece tu pesar, no ha atrapado
ese caliente palpitar de otro vuelo.
Mano volante perseguida: pareja.
Dulces, oscuras, apagadas, cruzáis.

Sois las amantes vocaciones, los signos
que en la tiniebla sin sonido se apelan.
Cielo extinguido de luceros que, tibio,
campo a los vuelos silenciosos te brindas.

Manos de amantes que murieron, recientes,
manos con vida que volantes se buscan
y cuando chocan y se estrechan encienden
sobre los hombres una luna instantánea.

Hands

See your hand, how slowly it moves,
transparent, tangible, pierced by light,
lovely, alive, nearly human in the night.
With the moon's reflection, with a painful cheek, with the
vagueness of dream See how it grows when you lift your arm,
fruitless search for a vanished night,
wing of light gliding silently
-and brushing against the dark vault.

Your grief gives off no glow, it hasn't caught
the other wing's warm heartbeat.
The pursuit of a flying hand: a couple.
Softly, darkly, gently, you encounter each other.

You are the occupation of lovers, signs
calling to each other silently in the dark.
Warm sky devoid of stars,
like a field you offer yourself to the silent wings.

Hands of lovers recently deceased,
living hands seeking each other in flight
collide and cling together igniting
a sudden moon above the world of men.

El Poeta

Para ti, que conoces cómo la piedra canta,
y cuya delicada pupila sabe ya del peso de una montaña
sobre un ojo dulce,
y cómo el resonante clamor de los bosques se aduerme
suave un día en nuestras venas;

para ti, poeta, que sentiste en tu aliento
la embestida brutal de las aves celestes,
y en cuyas palabras tan pronto vuelan las poderosas alas
de las águilas
como se ve brillar el lomo de los calientes peces sin sonido:

oye este libro que a tus manos envío
con ademán de selva,
pero donde de repente una gota tresquísima de rocío brilla
sobre una rosa,
o se ve batir el deseo del mundo,
la tristeza que como párpado doloroso
cierra el poniente y oculta el sol como una lágrima oscurecida,
mientras la inmensa frente fatigada
siente un beso sin luz, un beso largo,
unas palabras mudas que habla el mundo finando.

Sí, poeta: el amor y el dolor son tu reino.
Carne mortal la tuya, que, arrebatada por el espíritu,
arde en la noche o se eleva en el mediodía poderoso,
inmensa lengua profética que lamiendo los cielos
ilumina palabras que dan muerte a los hombres.

La juventud de tu corazón no es una playa

The Poet

For you, who know how the stone sings,
and whose delicate pupil knows a mountain's weight on a
loving eye, and how the forest's resounding echos softly
fall asleep in our veins one day;

for you, poet, whose breath felt
the celestial birds' brutal assault,
and whose words are traversed by the eagle's powerful wings
silently like the hot fishes' gleaming spine:

listen to this book conveyed by my hands
with jungle gestures,
but where a fresh dewdrop suddenly glistens on a rose,
or where the world's desire can be seen beating,
sadness that closes the west like a sorrowful eyelid
and conceals the sun like a hidden tear,
while an enormous exhausted forehead
feels a kiss without light, a long kiss,
a few mute words spoken by the dying world.

Yes, poet: love and pain are your kingdom.
Carried away by the spirit, your mortal flesh
blazes in the night or rises in the midday sun,
immense prophetic tongue licking the heaven
illuminating words that doom men to death.

Your heart's youthfulness is not a beach
where the sea charges with its foaming breakers,
love teeth biting the earth's edges,
softly bellowing at various beings.

donde la mar embiste con sus espumas rotas,
dientes de amor que mordiendo los bordes de la tierra,
braman dulce a los seres.

No es ese rayo velador que súbitamente te amenaza.
iluminando un instante tu frente desnuda,
para hundirse en tus ojos e incendiarte, abrasando
los espacios con tu vida que de amor se consume.

No. Esa luz que en el mundo
no es ceniza última,
luz que nunca se abate como polvo en los labios,
eres tú, poeta, cuya mano y no luna
yo vi en los cielos una noche brillando.

Un pecho robusto que reposa atravesado por el mar
respira como la inmensa marea celeste
y abre sus brazos yacentes y toca, acaricia
los extremos límites de la tierra.

¿Entonces?

Sí, poeta; arroja este libro que pretende encerrar en sus
páginas un destello del sol,
y mira a la luz cara a cara, apoyada la cabeza en la roca,
mientras tus pies remotísimos sienten el beso postrero del
poniente
y tus manos alzadas tocan dulce la luna,
y tu cabellera colgante deja estela en los astros.

And it is not the, vigilant lightning that suddenly threatens
you,
briefly illuminating your bare forehead,
sinking into your eyes and incinerating you, consuming
space and your life burning itself out from love.

No. This light that is not
the world's final ashes,
light that never loses heart like dust on someone's lips
is you, poet, whose hand and not the moon
I saw shining in the heavens one night.

A robust chest covered by the sea
breathes like the immense celestial tide
and opens its inert arms to touch, to caress
the earth's furthest frontiers.

And so?
Yes, poet; throw away this book whose pages pretend to
enclose a flash of sunlight,
and look in the light, face to face, with your head against a
rock,
while your remote feet feel the sun's last kiss
and your uplifted hands gently touch the moon,
and your long hair leaves a trail among the stars.

Louis Aragon

Born in Paris, Louis Aragon (1897–1982) was one of the original four Surrealist musketeers. Together with André Breton, Paul Eluard, and Philippe Soupault, he founded the French Surrealist movement in 1924. Originally a member of Paris Dada, like his three colleagues, he was a prolific writer, and published a volume every year during the 1920s. With the arrival of the following decade, as his Marxist sympathies grew more intense, Aragon distanced himself from his former friends, joined the French Communist Party, and, from then on, devoted himself entirely to leftist causes. Drafted in 1939, he was awarded the Croix de guerre and the military medal for acts of bravery. Following the Fall of France, in May 1940, he was active in the French Resistance, both through literary activities, and as an actual organizer of Resistance action. A popular poet in France, Aragon wrote many poems that have been set to music, and sung by various singers.

Mimosas

Le gouvernement venait de s'abattre
Dans un buisson d'aubépines
Une grève générale se découvrait à perte de vue
Sous les influences combinées de la lune et de la céphalagie
Les assassins s'enfuyaient dans la perspective des courants d'air
La victime pendait à la grille comme un bifteck
Une chaleur à claquer
Aussi faut voir si les casernes en entendaient de drôles
L'alcool coulait à flots par les tabatières des toits
Le métropolitain sortit de terre afin de respirer
Quand tout à coup il apparut
Au détour de la rue
Un petit âne qui traînait une voiture
Décorée pour la bataille des fleurs
Premier prix pour toute la ville
Et les villes voisines

Serrure De Sûreté

Ma parole
La main prise dans la porte
Trop engagé mon ami trop engagé
Pour ainsi dire
Ou
Passez-moi le mot
Merci
Je tiens la clef
Le verrou se remet à tourner comme une langue
Donc

Mimosas

The government had just collapsed
In a hawthorn bush
A general strike appeared as far as one could see
Under the combined influences of the moon and cephalalgia
The assassins fled in the breezes' perspective
The victim hung from the grill like a beefsteak
A clattering heat
Need to see if the barracks heard some amusing stories
Waves of alcohol were flowing by the roofs' snuff-boxes
The subway emerged from the ground to breathe
When all of a sudden there appeared
Where the street curved
A little donkey pulling a cart
Decorated for the war of the flowers
First prize for the whole town
And the neighboring towns

Safety Lock

My word
Hand caught in the door
Too busy my friend too busy
So to speak
Or
Pass me the word
Thank you
I am holding the key
The bolt resumes turning like a tongue
Therefore

Déclaration Définitive

Fais un trou dans ma pauvre
Poche
Mais mon chéri et ton trousseau
De clefs
Qu'il tombe le vampire
Dans le ruisseau la boue l'ordure
Tant pis si les balayeuses
Mécaniques
Passent par là traînant leurs jupes
Démodées
Si les flics efflanqués se foutent
La gueule par terre
Le pied pris dans l'anneau
Pour la sûreté des dites
Clefs
Tant pis si les dames d'un air
Désapprobateur
Verrouillent leurs portes métaphysiques
Sur mon passage
Car
Je n'aime que toi

Definitive Statement

Make a hole in my poor
Pocket
But my dear and your ring
Of keys
Let the vampire fall
In the gutter the mud the filth
Too bad if the mechanical
Street sweepers
Pass that way dragging their old-fashioned
Skirts
If the lanky cops throw
Their ugly mugs on the ground
Their feet caught in the ring
For the safety of the aforesaid
Keys
Too bad if the ladies who look
Disapprovingly
Bolt their metaphysical doors
When I pass by
For
I love only you

Partie Fine

Dans le coin où bouffent les évèques
Les notaires les maréchaux
On a écrit en lettres rouges
DÉGUSTATION D'HUÎTRES
Est-ce une allusion

On me fait remarquer que c'est pitoyable
Ce genre de plaisanterie
Et puis c'est mal foutu paraît-il
En temps que Poème
Car pour ce qui touche à la Poésie
On sait à quoi s'en tenir

Mais je n'ai pas fini de prendre en mauvaise part
Tout ce qui touche à la flicaille à la militairerie
Et plus particulièrement croa-croa aux curetages
J'en'ai pas assez le goût des alexandrins
Pour me le faire par-donner pan pan pan pan

Mais ici même si on ne sait d'où elle tombe
D'où tombe-t-elle d'ailleurs D'ailleurs
Il me plaît d'opposer à la clique des têtes à claques
Une femme très belle toute nue
Toute nue à ce point que ne n'en crois pas mes yeux

Bien que ce soit peut-être la millième fois
Que ce prodige s'offre à ma vue
Ma vue est à ses pieds
Son très humble serviteur

Fine Party

In the corner where the bishops the notaries the sergeants
Stuff their faces
Someone has written in red letters
OYSTER TASTING
Is it an allusion

They are right that this kind of joke
Is pitiful
And it is also poorly constructed it seems
If it is meant as a Poem
For as far as Poetry is concerned
I know a thing or two

I haven't finished thinking the worst of
Everything associated with cops with soldier boys
And more particularly caw caw on the curetages
I don't care enough about alexandrines
To ask for forgiveness bang bang bang bang

But even if no one knows where she comes from
Where does she come from moreover Moreover
It pleases me to juxtapose a gorgeous naked woman
With this bunch of ugly faces
So naked that I don't believe my eyes

Although this is perhaps the thousandth time
That this miracle presents itself to my sight
My sight is at her feet
Her very humble servant

Tercets

Le trousseau de clefs tout aux belles chimères
Se fredonnait
Une chanson du bon vieux temps

Pauvre insensé tu n'as pas vu l'autruche
Qui s'apprête bis à te dévorer
Pauvre insensé

Elle a lissé avec la brillantine
Son poil d'oiseau
Avec la brillantine

Et maintenant elle a l'air de quelque chose
L'oeil très intelligent
Le pied sûr comme une personne d'instruction

Qui dirait que dans sa patrie
On ne la considérait pas du tout
Les salons lui restaient lettre morte

Mais depuis qu'elle couche avec le parapluie
Tout le monde lui saute au cou
Elle sourit et dit Jolie parure

Le parapluie se frise la moustache
Et fait allusion à Joséphine de Beauharnais
Manière de se pousser du col

Dans une vie antérieure
Il aurait rêvé d'être pacha d'Egypte
Mais il se demande

Si dans une pareille aventure
Son harem aurait enfermé des houris ou des momies
Car il n'est pas très fixé sur l'Egypte

Tercets

The key ring with the beautiful chimeras
Was humming
A song from the good old days

Poor fool didn't you see the ostrich
That was preparing to devour you
Poor fool

With brilliantine she preened
Her feathers
With brilliantine

And now she looks better
With a very intelligent eye
With a sure foot like an instructor

Who would think that in her native land
No one thought very much of her
Fashonable salons were closed to her

But since she started sleeping with the umbella
Everyone throws their arms around her
She smiles and says Beautiful gown

The umbrella curls his mustache
And alludes to Josephine de Beauharnais
Has a way of pushing his neck forward

In an earlier life
He would have dreamed of being an Egyptian pasha
But he wonders

Given such an adventure
If his harem would have included houris or mummies
For he still has doubts about Egypt

Chanson À Boire

Si les verres étaient vraiment des verres
Et non des aérostats
Voguant la nuit vers les lèvres peintes
Les mains seraient-elles encore des oiseaux
Mains qui se ferment sur l'alcool

Mains qui étreignent le grisou
Les moutons qui paissent la nappe
N'ont pas peur des colombes à cause
De leur blancheur
Laisse-moi rire

Colombes vous n'êtes pas seulement redoutables
Pour le ballon captif qui me ressemble
Comme un frère mais
Aussi pour le plomb de la plaine

Regardez regardez comme les mains que j'aime
Au matin quand les enseignes lumineuses
Rivalisent encore avec l'aurore comme
Elles savent plier l'échine des moutons
Craquez vertèbres
Ah ah l'argenterie était fausse
Les cuillers comme des balles sont en plomb

Drinking Song

If water glasses were really water glasses
And not airships
Sailing at night toward painted lips
Hands would still be birds

Hands that close on alcohol
Hands that hug the fire-damp
The sheep grazing on the tablecloth
Do not fear the doves because
Of their whiteness
Let me laugh

Doves you not only threaten
The observation balloon that resembles me
Like a brother but
Also the leaden plain

Look look how the hands I love
In the morning when the illuminated signs
Still rival the dawn how
They bend the sheeps' spines
Crack vertebrae
Ah ah the silver-plate was false
The spoons are made of lead like bullets

Braulio Arenas

Born in La Serena, Chile, Braulio Arenas (1913–88) enrolled in law school in Santiago, but soon dropped out in order to devote himself to writing. In 1938, excited by what was transpiring in Europe, he founded the Surrealist group, Mandrágora, together with Teófilo Cid and Enrique Gómez Correa. They published a journal also called *Mandrágora*, from 1938 to 1941, and an anthology of poetry, *El A, G, C de la Mandrágora* (*The A,G, C of the Mandrake*), which included works by Arenas and Correa, but not Cid. Believing that *Mandrágora* had grown stale, Arenas broke with his friends, in 1942, founding another magazine called *Leitmotiv*. The author of numerous books of poetry, nine novels, and several collections of essays, Arenas received the Chilean Premio Nacional de Literatura in 1984.

Día A Día

El vidrio de la ventana se ha quebrado anticipadamente.
Unos decían: "Han sido los colores del prisma al atravesar
la noche para fijarse en el techo." Otros culpaban al pez
lápiz; otros, al pez carta; otros, al pez buzón.
Sólo que a la mañana siguiente el vidrio de la ventana
se veía intacto. Nada, ni la menor trizadura, ni el menor
color, ni el menor sello de correo.
Las olas del mar, como de costumbre.

Juegos De Dormitorio

La lámpara reía a los ángeles
Sangrando por las narices
La lámpara semejaba un cerezo
(Un cerezo no sé porqué)

Yo abrí los brazos como quien
Cierra con prisa una ventana
En un brazo aprendí a vivir

Yo dormía una bandada
De palomas voló de súbito
Estas palomas provenían
De un internado de hechiceras

Las jovencitas en corpiño
Frente al espejo alucinante
Se habían clavado la cabeza
Con un pernicioso alfiler negro

Day by Day

The window pane has shattered in anticipation. Some said: "It was the prism's colors that traversed the night and settled on the roof." Others blamed the pencil fish; others, the letter fish; others, the mailbox fish.
Except the next morning the window pane was discovered to be intact. Nothing, neither the tiniest piece, nor the tiniest color, nor the tiniest postage stamp.
The sea's waves, as usual.

Bedroom Games

The lamp was laughing at the angels
Who were suffering from nose-bleeds
The lamp appeared to be a cherry tree
(I don't know why a cherry tree)

I opened my arms like someone
Hurriedly closing a window
I learned to swim in an arm
I learned to live in a kiss

I was sleeping a flock
Of doves suddenly flew away
These doves came
From a witches' boarding school

The little girls in brassierees
Facing the hallucinatory mirror
Had stuck pernicioius, black pins
In their heads

Pronto en palomas convertidas
Por este infantil acto mágico
Salieron volando por el cielo
Rumbo a mi abierto dormitorio

Yo dormía como quien
Vive una noche para siempre
La noche semejaba un alfiler
(Un alfiler no sé porqué)

Cáceres

Sin recurrir a las ventanas
Sin asomarse a las panoplias
Sin colgar frutos de los árboles
Sin cortar en dos la noche
Sin esperar el buen consejo
Sin recurrir a las ventanas
Sin propender a los relámpagos
Sin asomarse a las panoplias
Sin atisbar el mes de enero
Sin decidirse a abrir la puerta
Cuando se fue Jorge de viaje

Suddenly transformed into doves
By this childish magic act
They flew off into the sky
Heading for my open bedroom

I was sleeping like someone
Living a night forever
The night appeared to be a pin
(I don't know why a pin)

Cáceres

Without resorting to the windows
Without glancing at the collection of arms
Without hanging fruit on the trees
Without cutting the night in two
Without hoping for good advice
Without resorting to the windows
Without tending toward flashes of lightning
Without glancing at the collection of arms
Without watching for the month of January
Without deciding to open the door
When Jorge left on a trip

Hechos Diversos

El mar, el mar dormía de proa y se llenaba el cuerpo de tierra.
Lejos
estaban ya los últimos escándalos del faro, la noche fratricida y
aquel
regreso en la imperial del tranvía.
El mar recuperaba su vigor, su estrecho de Torres, y lanzaba sus
icebergs
en contra de los balleneros.
En los muros florecía la vellorita, y las ventanas de la casa
ostentaban
herméticos blasones de una complicada simetría.
La lluvia caía a torrentes para usucapir el mar, y la trama de la
selva estaba
rota en mil pedazos.
Inútil concordancia, los relámpagos nubios sacuden los desiertos
libertinos,
la hora avanza, la hora más negra de la cual me he burlado
siempre.

El Corazón

Tú hablaste del corazón hasta por los ojos
Tú hablaste del fuego hasta por la nieve
Por ti yo un día me decidí al azar
Para encontrarte

Yo he desatado el nudo del azar
Una mañana me decidí de súbito
Y sólo quien haya logrado desatarlo
Podrá entenderme

Various Acts

The sea, the sea was sleeping on its prow and was filling its body
with earth.
The lighthouse's last scandals were already nearly forgotten, with
the
fratricidal night and the return home on the steetcar's upper deck.
The sea was regaining its vigor, its Torres Straits, and was
launching its
icebergs against the whalers.
Daisies were flowering on the walls, and the house's windows
sported
hermetic coats of arms with a complicated symmetry.
The rain was falling in torrents in order to acquire title to the sea,
and the
jungle's weaving was broken into a thousand pieces.
Useless agreement, the Nubian lightning fllashes jolt the libertine
deserts,
the hour advances, the blackest hour which I have always
ridiculed.

The Heart

You spoke of the heart even through your eyes
You spoke of fire even through the snow
For you I decided by chance one day
To meet you

I have untied the knot of chance
One morning I suddenly decided
And only someone who has managed to untie it
Will understand me

Yo he desatado el nudo del azar
Un nudo astuto viejo y persistente
Y esta tarea era semejante
        A la belleza

Yo he desatado el nudo del azar
Y tú mujer apareciste entonces
Mujer azar y azar mujer eran en todo
        Tan semejantes

Tantas Lunas

Tantas lunas pasadas en limpio
Rayas y más rayas tigres y más tigres
Y el hotel era lujoso para dormir

Sueños y más sueños besos y más besos
Qué quedará de tanta luna
Qué quedará de tanta agua de tanta sed de tanto vaso

Ventana destinada para ti
Para que en ella te apoyes más perfecta
Tú haces con tu belleza
Lo que otros hacen con el cielo

I have untied the knot of chance
A clever old and persistent knot
And this task was similar
　　To beauty

I have untied the knot of chance
And then you appeared woman
Woman chance and chance woman were basically
　　So alike

So Many Moons

So many moons come and gone
Stripes and more stripes tigers and more tigers
And the luxury hotel to sleep in

Dreams and more dreams kisses and more kisses
What will remain of so much moon
What will remain of so much water so much thirst
　　so much drinking glass

Window destined for you
So you can depend on it more perfect
You make of your beauty
What others make of the sky

Poema De Memoria

Para embellecer al cerezo
Con un papiro nigromántico
Esta mañana se ha vestido
Una silente alondra roja

Yo llevé esta alondra un día
Entre mis manos enguantadas
Hasta un Café en el que solía
Reunirme con mis amigos

Lejano tiempo ya el cerezo
Se tumbó al ímpetu del hacha
La alondra roja es un recuerdo
En mi vida de un solo día

Esta mañana se ha vestido
Con un papiro nigromántico
Una silente alondra roja
Para embellecer al cerezo

Poem From Memory

To adorn the cherry tree
With a necromantic papyrus
The morning has dressed itself in
A silent, red lark

One day I carried the lark
In my gloved hands
To a Café where I used
To meet my friends

Many years ago the cherry tree
Was felled by the axe's momentum
The red lark is a memory
Of a single day in my life

The morning has dressed itself
In a necromantic papyrus
A silent, red lark
To adorn the cherry tree

Antonin Artaud

Antonin Artaud (1896–1948) suffered from acute schizophrenia, punctuated by psychotic episodes, for much of his life. Born in Marseille, he arrived in Paris in 1920, and discovered a love of the theater. While pursuing an acting career, Artaud continued to write both poetry and essays. Joining the Surrealist group in 1924, he participated in many of its activities, and became interested in contemporary cinema. Over the next few years, he co-founded the Théâtre Alfred Jarry with Roger Vitrac, and Robert Aron (1926), wrote the scenario for the first Surrealist movie: *La Coquille et le clergyman* (*The Seashell and the Clergyman*) (1928), and acted in Abel Gance's *Napoléon* (1927) and Carl Theodor Dreyer's *La Passion de Jeanne d'Arc* (1928). In 1931, inspired by a Balinese dance troupe, Artaud's proposal to create a "Theater of Cruelty" was later incorporated into *Le Théâtre et son double* (1938).

Une Grande Ferveur …

Une grande ferveur pensante et surpeuplée portait mon moi comme un abîme plein. Un vent charnel et résonnant soufflait, et le soufre même en était dense. Et des radicelles infimes peuplaient ce vent comme un réseau de veines, et leur entrecroisement fulgurait. L'espace était mesurable et crissant, mais sans forme pénétrable. Et le centre était une mosaïque d'éclats, une espèce de dur marteau cosmique, d'une lourdeur défigurée, et qui retombait sans cesse comme un front dans l'espace, mais avec un bruit comme distillé. Et l'enveloppement cotonneux du bruit avait l'instance obtuse et la pénétration d'un regard vivant. Oui, l'espace rendait son plein coton mental où nulle pensée encore n'était nette et ne restituait sa décharge d'objets. Mais, peu à peu, la masse tourna comme une nausée limoneuse et puissante, une espèce d'immense influx de sang végétal et tonnant. Et les radicelles qui tremblaient à la lisière de mon oeil mental, se détachèrent avec une vitesse de vertige de la masse crispée du vent. Et tout l'espace trembla comme un sexe que le globe du ciel ardent saccageait. Et quelque chose du bec d'une colombe réelle troua la masse confuse des états, toute la pensée profonde à ce moment se stratifiait, se résolvait, devenait transparente et réduite.

Et il nous fallait maintenant une main qui devînt l'organe même du saisir. Et deux ou trois fois encore la masse entière et végétale tourna, et chaque fois, mon oeil se replacait sur une position plus précise. L'obscurité elle-même devenait profuse et sans objet. Le gel entier gagnait la clarté.

A Great Fervor …

A great thoughtful fervor, and overpopulated, transported my ego like a full abyss. A carnal, resonant wind was blowing, and even its sulphur was dense. And some tiny rootlets populated this wind like a network of veins, and where they crossed there was a flash. The space was measurable and rasping, but without penetrable form. And the center was a mosaic of flashes, a kind of hard cosmic hammer, of a disfigured heaviness, which fell again and again like a forehead in the space, but with a noise that was practically distilled. And the noise's cottony envelope had the obtuse solicitation and the penetration of a living gaze. Yes, the space yielded its full mental cotton where no thought so far was clear and did not return its output of objects. But, little by little, the mass revolved like a muddy, powerful nausea, a kind of immense influx of vegetal, thundering blood. And the rootlets that were trembling on the edge of my mental eye, detached themselves with dizzying rapidity from the wind's contorted mass. And the whole space trembled like a sex that the ardent sky's globe was plundering. And something from a real dove's beak perforated the states' confused mass, the whole profound thought crystalized into layers at this moment, was resolved, and became transparent and smaller.

And now we needed a hand that would become the very organ of seizure. And the whole vegetal mass revolved two or three more times, and each time my eye repositioned itself more precisely. The very darkness became profuse and with no purpose. The frost all managed to reach the light.

Poète Noir

Poète noir, un sein de pucelle
te hante,
poète aigri, la vie bout
et la ville brûle,
et le ciel se résorbe en pluie,
ta plume gratte au coeur de la vie.

Forêt, forêt, des yeux fourmillent
sur les pinons multipliés;
cheveux d'orage, les poètes
enfourchent des chevaux, des chiens.

Les yeux ragent, les langues tournent
le ciel afflue dans les narines
comme un lait nourricier et bleu;
je suis suspendu à vos bouches
femmes, coeurs de vinaigre durs.

Avec Moi Dieu-Le-Chien …

Avec moi dieu-le-chien, et sa langue
qui comme un trait perce la croûte
de la double calotte en voûte
de la terre qui le démange.

Et voici le triangle d'eau
qui marche d'un pas de punaise,
mais qui sous la punaise en braise
se retourne en coup de couteau.

Black Poet

Black poet, haunted by
a maiden's breast,
embittered poet, life is boiling
and the town is burning,
and the sky is reabsorbed as rain,
your pen scratches at the heart of life.

Forest, forest, eyes are swarming
on the multiple pinions;
stormy hair, the poets
climb onto horses, dogs.

Their eyes rage, their tongues turn
the sky flows into their nostrils
like a nutritious blue milk;
I am hanging on your mouths
women, hard vinegar hearts.

With me God-The-Dog …

With me god-the-dog, and his tongue
like an arrow piercing the crust
of the earth's doubly vaulted skullcap
which makes him itch all over.

Behold the triangle of water
walking at a bedbug's pace,
but which turns around like a flashing knife
beneath the bedbug's red rug.

Sous les seins de la terre hideuse
dieu-la-chienne s'est retirée,
des seins de terre et d'eau gelée
qui pourrissent sa langue creuse.

Et voici la vierge-au-mareau,
pour broyer les caves de terre
dont le crâne du chien stellaire
sent monter l'horrible niveau.

Nuit

Les zincs passent dans les égouts,
la pluie remonte dans la lune;
dans l'avenue une fenêtre
nous découvre une femme nue.

Dans les outres des draps gonflés
où la nuit entière respire,
le poète sent ses cheveux
grandir et se multiplier.

La face obtuse des plafonds
contemple les corps allongés
entre le ciel et les pavés,
la vie est un repas profond.

Poète, ce qui te travaille
n'a rien à voir avec la lune;
la pluie est fraîche,
le ventre est bon.

God-the-bitch has retired
beneath the hideous earth's breasts,
breasts of earth and frozen water
that rot his hollow tongue.

And behold the virgin-with-hammer,
for grinding the earthen cellars
whose horrible rising water
the stellar dog's skull smells.

Night

The zinc counters disappear into the sewers,
the rain returns to the moon;
in the avenue a window
discloses a naked woman.

In the swollen sheets' goat-skin bottles
where the whole night respires,
the poet feels his hair
growing longer and multiplying.

The ceilings' obtuse faces
contemplate the bodies stretching
between the sky and the pavement,
life is a profound repast.

Poet, the source of your worries
has nothing to do with the moon;
the rain is cool,
your stomach is good.

Vois comme montent les verres
sur tous les comptoirs de la terre;
la vie est vide,
la tête est loin.

Quelque part un poète pense.
Nous n'avons pas besoin de lune,
la tête est grande,
le monde est plein.

dans chaque chambre
le monde tremble,
la vie accouche quelque chose
qui remonte vers les plafonds.

Un jeu de cartes flotte dans l'air
autour des verres;
fumée des vins, fumées des vers,
et des pipes de la soirée.

Dans l'angle oblique des plafonds
de toutes les chambres qui tremblent
s'amassent les fumées marines
des rêves mal échafaudés.

Car ici la vie est en cause
et le ventre de la pensée;
les bouteilles heurtent les crânes
de l'aérienne assemblée.

Le Verbe pousse du sommeil
comme une fleur, ou comme un verre
plein de formes et de fumées.

See how the glasses on every counter
suddenly rise into the air;
life is empty,
your head is distant.

Somewhere a poet is thinking.
We don't need a moon,
my head is large,
the world is full.

In each room
the world trembles,
life gives birth to something
that rises toward the ceiling.

A pack of cards floats in the air
around the glasses;
fumes from wine, from verses,
and from pipes in the evening.

In all the trembling rooms,
the marine fumes of poorly
constructed dreams collect in
their ceilings' obtuse angles.

For life is concerned here
and the stomach of thought;
bottles strike the skulls
of the aerial gathering.

The Word sprouts sleep
like a flower, or like a glass
filled with forms and fumes.

Le verre et le ventre se heurtent;
la vie est claire
dans les crânes vitrifiées.

L'aréopage ardent des poètes
s'assemble autour du tapis vert,
le vide tourne.

La vie traverse la pensée
du poète aux cheveux épais.

Dans la rue rien qu'une fenêtre;
les cartes battent,
dans la fenêtre la femme au sexe
met son ventre en délibéré.

Glass and the stomach knock together;
life is clear
in the vitrified skulls.

The poets' ardent tribunal
assembles around the green baize,
the void spins round and round.

Life traverses the poet's thought,
the poet with the thick hair.

In the street nothing but a window;
the cards are being shuffled,
in the window the woman
deliberately exposes her sex.

André Breton

André Breton (1896–1966) was the founder, theoretician, and animator of the French Surrealist movement. The author of a great many poems, several manifestos, and numerous critical essays, he collaborated with Philippe Soupault on what is probably the first Surrealist text: *Les Champs magnétiques* (*Magnetic Fields*) (1919). Born in a small town in Normandy, Breton went on to study medicine in Paris, but he was drafted into the army in 1915. Assigned to various neuro-psychiatric centers, he learned about Sigmund Freud's theories and devoted the rest of his life to exploring the human psyche. Persuaded that "l'existence est ailleurs" ("existence is elsewhere"), as he proclaimed in the *First Surrealist Manifesto* (1924), Breton strove to unite the conscious with the unconscious using all the tools at his disposal.

Tournesol

à Pierre Reverdy

La voyageuse qui traversa les Halles à la tombée de l'été
Marchait sur la pointe des pieds
le désespoir roulait au ciel ses grands arums; si beaux
Et dans le sac à main il y avait mon rêve ce flacon de sels
Que seule a respirés la marraine de Dieu
Les torpeurs se déployaient comme la buée
Au Chien qui fume
Où venaient d'entrer le pour et le contre
La jeune femme ne pouvait être vue d'eux que mal et de biais
Avais-je affaire à l'ambassadrice du salpêtre
Ou de la courbe blanche sur fond noir que nous appelons pensée
Le bal des innocents battait son plein
Les lampions prenaient feu lentement dans les marronniers
La dame sans ombre s'agenouilla sur le Pont au Change
Rue Git-le-Coeur les timbres n'étaient plus les mêmes
Les promesses des nuits étaient enfin tenues
Les pigeons voyageurs les baisers de secours
Se joignaient aux seins de la belle inconnue
Dardés sous le crêpe des significations parfàites
Une ferme prospérait en plein Paris
Et ses fenêtres donnaient sur la voie lactée
Mais personne ne l'habitait encore à cause des survenants;
Des survenants qu'on sait plus dévoués que les revenants
Les uns comme cette femme ont l'air de nager
Et dans l'amour il entre un peu de leur substance
Elle les intériorise
Je ne suis le jouet d'aucune puissance sensorielle
Et pourtant le grillon qui chantait dans les cheveux de cendre
Un soir près de la statue d'Etienne Marcel
M'a jeté un coup d'oeil d'intelligence
André Breton a-t-il dit passe

Sunflower

For Pierre Reverdy

The female explorer who traversed Les Halles market at summer's fall
Was walking on tiptoe
Despair revolved its great lovely calla lilies in the sky
And in her handbag was my dream that flask of salts
That only God's fairy godmother has inhaled
Torpors unfurled themselves like the mist
From the café called The Smoking Dog
Where pro and con had just entered
The young woman could barely be seen by them diagonally
Was I dealing with the ambassadress with saltpeter
Or of the white curve on a black background that we call thought
The innocents' ball was in full swing
The Chinese lanterns slowly caught fire in the chestnut trees
The shadowless lady knelt on the Pont-au-Change bridge
In the Rue Gît-le-Coeur the sounds of the bells were different
The nights' promises were observed at last
Homing pigeons emergency kisses
Converged on the beautiful stranger's breasts
Jutting out beneath the silk of perfect meanings
A farm prospered in the middle of Paris
And its windows looked out on the Milky Way
But nobody yet inhabited it because of last-minute guests
Unexpected guests that are known to be more devoted than ghosts
Some of them like that woman appear to be swimming
And in love there enters a little of their substance
She assimilates them
I am not the plaything of any sensory power
And yet the cricket who was singing in the ashen hair
One evening near the statue of Etienne Marcel
-Winked at me slyly
André Breton he said you may pass

Le Grand Secours Meurtrier

La statue de Lautréamont
Au socle de cachets de quinine
En rase campagne
L'auteur des Poésies est couché à plat ventre
Et près de lui veille l'héloderme suspect
Son oreille gauche appliquée au sol est une boite vitrée
Occupée par un éclair l'artiste n'a pas oublié de faire figurer
au-dessus de lui
Le ballon bleu ciel en forme de tète de Turc
Le cygne de Montevideo dont les ailes sont déployées et toujours
prêtes à battre
Lorsqu'il s'agit d'attirer de l'horizon les autres cygnes
Ouvre sur le faux univers deux yeux de couleurs différentes
L'un de sulfate de fer sur la treille des as l'autre de boue diamantée
Il voit le grand hexagone à entonnoir dans lequel se crisperont
bientôt
les machines
Que l'homme s'acharne à couvrir de pansements
Il ravive de sa bougie de radium les fonds du creuset humain
Le sexe de plumes le cerveau de papier huilé
Il préside aux cérémonies deux fois nocturnes qui ont pour but
soustraction
faite du feu d'intervertir les coeurs de l'homme et de l'oiseau
J'ai accès près de lui en qualité de convulsionnaire
Les femmes ravissantes qui m'introduisent dans le wagon
capitonné de roses
Où un hamac qu'elles ont pris soin de me faire de leurs
chevelures m'est réservé
De toute éternité
Me recommandent avant de partir de ne pas prendre froid dans
la lecture
du journal
Il parait que la statue près de laquelle le chiendent de mes
terminaisons nerveuses
Arrive à destination est accordée chaque nuit comme un piano

Lethal Release

Lautreamont's statue
On a pedestal made of quinine tablets
In the countryside
The author of the *Poems* is lying face down
And the questionable Gila monster is watching nearby
His left ear to the ground is a glass box
Occupied by a lightning flash the artist did not forget to depict
The sky-blue ballon above him shaped like a Turk's head knot
The Swan of Montevideo whose wings are extended and
  preparing to flap
When he wishes to attract – other swans from the horizon
Opens two eyes of different colors on the false universe
One of iron sulfate against the eyelashes' trellis the other of mud
  set
with diamonds
He sees the large hexagonal funnel in which machines will soon
  shrivel
That mankind persists in covering with bandages
With his radium candle he revives the depths of the human
  crucible
The feathered genitals the oilcloth brain
He presides over doubly nocturnal rites intended to transpose
  the hearts
of man and bird without fire
In my convulsionary capacity I am able to approach him
The ravishing women who usher me into the railroad car
  uphostered with roses
Where a hamock they have fabricated with their hair is reserved
  for me
For all eternity
Advise me before leaving not to catch a chill in reading the
  newspaper
It appears that the statue which the crabgrass of my nerve
  endings has chosen as its destination
Is tuned every night like a piano

Le Sphinx Vertebral

La belle ombre patiente et courbe fait le tour des pavés
Les fenêtres vénitiennes s'ouvrent et se ferment sur la place
Où vont en liberté des bêtes suivies de feux
Les réverbères mouillés bruissent encadrés d'une nuée d'yeux
bleus
Qui couvrent le paysage en amont de la ville
Ce matin proue du soleil comme tu t'engloutis dans les superbes
chants
exhalés à l'ancienne derrière les rideaux par les guetteuses nues
Tandis que les arums géants tournent autour de leur taille
Et que le mannequin sanglant saute sur ses trois pieds dans le
grenier
Il vient disent-elles en cambrant leur cou sur lequel le
bondissement des
nattes libère des glaciers à peine roses
Qui se fendent sous le poids d'un rai de lumière tombant des
persiennes arrachées
Il vient c'est le loup aux dents de verre
Celui qui mange l'heure dans les petites boites rondes
Celui qui souffle les parfums trop pénétrants des herbes
Celui qui fume les petits feux de passage le soir dans les navets
Les colonnes des grands appartements de marbre et de vétiver
crient
Elles crient elles sont prises de ces mouvements de va-et-vient
qui n'animaient
jusque-là que certaines pièces colossales des usines
Les femmes immobiles sur les plaques tournantes vont voir
Il fait jour à gauche mais nuit complètement nuit à droite

The Vertebral Sphinx

Patient and curved the beautiful shadow walks around the paving
stones
The Venetian windows open and close upon the public square
Where beasts roam freely followed by fires
The wet streetlights buzz framed by a cloud of blue eyes
That cover the landscape uphill from the town
This morning the sun's prow how you sink into the superb songs
sung
in the ancient mode by naked women peering from behind the
curtains
While the giant calla lilies revolve around their waist
And the bloody mannequin hops on its three feet in the attic
He is coming they say arching their necks whose bouncing braids
liberate glaciers
with a hint of rose
That split beneath the weight of a ray of light falling from the
torn Venetian blinds
He is coming it's the wolf with glass teeth
Who eats up time in little round cans
Who breathes the herbs' suffocating perfumes
Who smokes the little bonfires in the evening among the turnips
The columns of great apartments of marble and of vetiver plants
cry out
They cry they are possessed by back-and-forth movements
previously
restricted to certain huge factory parts
The immobile women on the turntables go to look
It is daylight on the left but night on the right night completely

Il y a des branchages encore pleins d'oiseaux qui passent à toute
allure
obscurcissant le trou de la croisée
Des oiseaux blancs qui pondent des oeufs noirs
Où sont ces oiseaux que remplacent maintenant des étoiles
bordées de
deux rangs de perles
Une tête de poisson très très longue ce n'est pas encore lui
De la tête de poisson naissent des jeunes filles secouant un tamis
Et du tamis des coeurs faits de larmes bataviques
Il vient c'est le loup aux dents de verre
Celui qui volait très haut sur les terrains vagues reparus
au-dessus des maisons
Avec des plantes aiguisées toutes tournées vers ses yeux
D'un vert à défier une bouteille de mousse renversée sur la neige
Ses griffes de jade dans lesquelles il se mire en volant
Son poil de la couleur des étincelles
C'est lui qui gronde dans les forges au crépuscule et dans les
lingeries
abandonnées
Il est visible on le touche il avance avec son balancier sur le fil
tendu d'hirondelles
Les guetteuses se penchent se penchent aux fenêtres
De tout leur côté d'ombre de tout leur côté de lumière
La bobine du jour est tirée par petits coups du côté du paradis de
sable
Les pédales de la nuit bougent sans interruption

There are branches heaped with birds that zoom past obscuring
the
casement window's opening
White birds that lay black eggs
Where are those birds now replaced by stars edged with two rows
of pearls
A very very long fish head he isn't here yet
From the fish head several girls emerge shaking a sieve
And from the sieve hearts made of glass tears
He is coming it's the wolf with glass teeth
Who flew very high over the wastelands that reappeared above
the houses
With sharpened plants all turned toward his eyes
Of a green to challenge a bottle of moss overturned on the snow
His jade claws in which he admires his reflection in mid flight
His fur the color of sparks
It is he who growls in the forges at dusk and in the abandoned
linen-rooms
He is visible someone touches him he advances with his
balancing pole
along the wire strung with swallows
The curious women lean out lean out of the windows
In the shadows in the light
The day's spool unwinds bit by bit toward the side of the sand
paradise
The night's treadles continue without interruption

Le Marquis De Sade …

Le marquis de Sade a regagné l'intérieur du volcan en éruption
D'où il était venu
Avec ses belles mains encore frangées
Ses yeux de jeune fille
Et cette raison à fleur de sauve-qui-peut qui ne fut
Qu'à lui
Mais du salon phosphorescent à lampes de viscères
Il n'a cessé de jeter les ordres mystérieux
Qui ouvrent une brèche dans la nuit morale
C'est par cette brèche que je vois
Les grandes ombres craquantes la vieille écorce minée
Se dissoudre
Pour me permettre de t'aimer
Comme le premier homme aima la première femme
En toute liberté
Cette liberté
Pour laquelle le feu même s'est fait homme
Pour laquelle le marquis de Sade défia les siècles de ses grands
   arbres abstraits
D'acrobates tragiques
Cramponnés au fil de la Vierge du désir

The Marquis De Sade …

The Marquis de Sade has gone back inside the erupting volcano
From which he had come
With his beautiful hands in ruffled cuffs
His girlish eyes
And that mentality on the edge of headlong flight which was
His alone
But from the phosphorescent salon with visceral lamps
He has not ceased to hurl mysterious orders
That open a breach in the moral night
Through that breach I see
The great cracking shadows the old rotten bark
Dissolve
Allowing me to love you
As the first man loved the first woman
In complete freedom
That freedom
For which fire itself became man
For which the Marquis de Sade defied the centuries with his great
abstract trees
With tragic acrobats
Clinging to the gossamer thread of desire

Le Puits Enchanté

Du dehors l'air est à se refroidir
Le feu éteint sous la bouillotte bleue des bois

La nature crache dans sa petite boîte de nuit
Sa brosse sans épaisseur commence à faire luire les arêtes des buissons et des navires

La ville aux longues aiguillées de fulgores
Monte jusqu'à se perdre
Le long d'une rampe de chansons qui tourne en vrille dans les rues désertes

Quand les marelles abandonnées se retournent l'une après l'autre dans le ciel

Tout au fond de l'entonnoir
Dans les fougères foulés du regard

J'ai rendez-vous avec la dame du lac

Je sais qu'elle viendra
Comme si je m'étais endormi sous des fuchsias

C'est là
A la place de la suspension du dessous dans la maison des nuages

Une cage d'ascenseur aux parois de laquelle éclatent par touffes du linge de femme
De plus en plus vert

A moi

A moi la fleur du grisou
le ludion humain la roussette blanche
La grande devinette sacrée

Mieux qu'au fil de l'eau Ophélie au ballet des mouches de mai
Voici au reflet du fil à plomb celle qui est dans le secret des taupes

The Enchanted Well

Outside the air is growing colder
The fire extinguished beneath the woods' blue hotwater bottle

Nature spits into its little night box
Its thin brush begins to make the bushes' and the ships'
bones glisten

The town with long needlefuls of fireflies
Rises to the point of vanishing
Along a ramp of songs that spirals down the deserted streets

When abandoned hopscotch squares turn over one after
another in the sky
At the funnel's very bottom

In the glance's trampled ferns
I have a rendezvous with the lady of the lake.

I know she will come
As if I had fallen asleep beneath some fuchsias
It is there
At the place where the house of clouds' underpinnings are
suspended

An elevator cage whose walls are bursting with tufts of
women's lingerie
Greener and greener

Mine
Mine the fire-damp's flower
The human bottle-diver the white fruit-bat
The great sacred riddle

Better than Ophelia with the flow at the mayflies' ballet
Observe in the plumbline's reflection she who knows the
moles' secrets

I see the sole of diamond dust I see the white peacock who
spreads his tail

Je vois la semelle de poussière de diamant je vois le paon blanc qui fait la roue
derrière l'écran de la cheminée

Les femmes qu'on dessine à l'envers sont les seules qu'on n'ait jamais vues

Son sourire est fait pour l'expiation des plongeurs de perles
Aux poumons changés en coraux

C'est Méduse casquée dont le buste pivote lentement dans la vitrine
De profil je caresse ses seins aux pointes ailées

Ma voix ne lui parviendrait pas ce sont deux mondes
Et même
Rien ne servirait de jeter dans sa tour une lettre toute ouverte aux angles de glu

On m'a passé les menottes étincelantes de Peter Ibbetson

Je suis un couvreur devenu fou
Qui arrache par plaques et finirai bien par jeter bas tout le toit de la maison
Pour mieux voir comme la trombe s'élève de la mer
Pour me mêler à la bataille de fleurs
Quand une cuisse déborde l'écrin et qu'entre en jeu la pédale du danger

La belle invention
Pour remplacer le coucou l'horloge à escarpolette
Qui marque le temps suspendu

Pendeloque du lustre central de la terre
Mon sablier de roses
Toi qui ne remonterais pas à la surface
Toi qui me regardes sans me voir dans les jardins de la provocation pure
Toi qui m'envoies un baiser de la portière d'un train qui fuit

behind the fireplace screen

Only women who are sketched backwards have never been
seen

Her smile is destined for the atonement of pearl divers
Whose lungs are changed to coral

It is helmeted Medusa whose bust revolves slowly in the
shop window
Sideways I caress her breasts with winged nipples

My voice would never reach her they are two different
worlds

And even
It would serve no purpose to throw into her tower a
wide-open letter with
bird-lime corners

They put Petter Ibbetson's dazzling handcuffs on me

I am a roofer who has gone mad
Who rips up layers and will finally destroy the house's
entire roof
To better observe the waterspout rising from the sea
To involve myself in the battle of the flowers
When a thigh overflows the jewel case and danger's pedal
comes into play

A beautiful invention
To replace the cuckoo the clock with a child's swing
That records suspended time

Crystal pendant of the earth's central chandelier
My hourglass of roses
You who will not rise to the surface
You who observe me without seeng me in the gardens of
pure provocation
You who blow me a kiss from the door of a fleeing train

Femme Et Oiseau

Le chat rêve et ronronne dans la lutherie brune. Il scrute le fond de l'ébène et de biais lape à distance le tout vif acajou. C'est l'heure où le sphinx de la garance détend par milliers sa trompe autour de la fontaine de Vaucluse et où partout la femme n'est plus qu'un calice débordant de voyelles en liaison avec le magnolia illimitable de la nuit.

Le Bel Oiseau Déchiffrant L'Inconnu Au Couple D'amoureux

Les bancs des boulevards extérieurs s'infléchissent avec le temps sous l'étreinte des lianes qui s'étoilent tout bas de beaux yeux et de lèvres. Alors qu'ils nous paraissent libres continuent autour d'eux à voleter et fondre les unes sur les autres ces fleurs ardentes. Elles sont pour nous traduire en termes concrets l'adage des mythographes qui veut que l'attraction universelle soit une qualité de l'espace et l'attraction charnelle la fille de cette qualité mais oublie par trop de spécifier que c'est ici à la fille, pour le bal, de parer la mère. Il suffit d'un souffle pour libérer ces myriades d'aigrettes porteuses d'akènes. Entre leur essor et leur retombée selon la courbe sans fin du désir s'inscrivent en harmonie tous les signes qu'englobe la partition céleste.

Woman and Bird

The cat is dreaming and purring in the brown stringed-instrument shop. It scrutinizes the depth of the ebony and from a distance laps the living mahogany obliquely. It is the hour when the madderwort sphinx loosens by the thousands her hunting horn around the fountain of Vaucluse and when woman everywhere becomes a chalice overflowing with vowels in connection with the illimitable magnolia of the night.

The Lovely Bird Deciphering the Unknown For a Pair of Lovers

In time the benches on the outer boulevards sag beneath the embrace of vines that are softly starred with beautiful eyes and lips. Although they appear care-free to us, these ardent flowers continue to flutter around and to swoop down on each other. They are to translate ourselves into concrete terms the adage of mythographers who claim that gravitational attraction is a characteristic of space and carnal attraction the daughter of that characteristic but which completely neglects to specify that it is the daughter's turn, for the ball, to help her mother dress. A single breath suffices to liberate those myriads of egrets bearing achene berries. Between their soaring flight and their descent along the endless curve of desire all the signs encompassed in the celestial score are inscribed harmoniously.

ANDRÉ BRETON, RENÉ CHAR, AND PAUL ELUARD

Au Fer Rouge

Le regard qui jettera sur mes épaules
Le filet indéchiffrable de la nuit
Sera comme une pluie d'éclipse
Il descendra lentement de son cadre solaire
Mes bras autour de son cou

Page Blanche

Le marbre des palais est aujourd'hui plus dur que le soleil
Première proposition

La seconde est un peu moins bête
Le jeûne des vampires aura pour conséquence la soif qu'a le sang
d'être bu
La soif qu'a le sang d'épouser la forme des ruisseaux
La soif qu'a le sang de jaillir dans les endroits déserts

La soif qu'a le sang de l'eau fraîche du couteau
Le corps et l'âme sont réunis par une accolade
Troisième proposition celle-ci de caractère malhonnête
Parce que le corps et l'âme se compromettent ensemble
Parce qu'ils se servent d'excuse l'un à l'autre

With a Red-Hot Iron

The glance that will cover my shoulders
With the night's indecipherable net
Will be like a rain of eclipse
It will descend slowly from its solar frame
My arms around its neck

Blank Page

Today the palaces' marble is harder than the sun
First proposition

The second is not quite so stupid
The vampires' fasting will bring about the blood's thirst to be
drunk
The blood's thirst to adopt the gutters' form
The blood's thirst to gush forth in deserted places

The blood's thirst for the knife's cold water
Body and soul are reunited in an embrace
Third proposition of a dishonest nature
Because body and soul compromise one another together
Because each serves as an excuse for the other

À La Promenade

Nous sommes passés devant la pharmacie
Les bocaux étaient le jour et la nuit
On apportait un blessé
Et dans le rassemblement il y avait une femme qui chantait
Un bouquet fané sur l'oreille
Son visage était une grande place déserte
Que l'ivresse murait
Et que cherchaient des bohémiennes
Sa chanson nous apportait les bribes de notre vie
A venir
Il flottait une terrible odeur de foin coupé
Mais les autres n'entendaient rien ne sentaient rien
Leur foule était un train bloqué par mille coups de sifflet
Un train bloqué par la folie sans corps
Un grand mystère comme un enfant perdu
Avec ces larmes sales qui voudraient être du sang
Et qui ne sont que de l'avoine
Fermez toutes les portes et toutes les fenêtres
Que personne ne sorte
Les signaux fonctionnent-ils
Cette femme où nous emmène-t-elle
La pharmacie madréporique s'effondre
La femme crache sur le blessé
Des buissons d'amoureux jettent au feu leurs fleurs d'amour

Insoumission du déjà-vu

Out For a Stroll

We passed by the pharmacy
The wide-mouthed jars were day and night
They brought in somebody injured
And a woman in the crowd was singing
With a faded bouquet behind her ear
Her face was a large, deserted public square
Which ecstasy was causing to ripen
And which some gypsies were seeking
Her song brought us snatches of our life
In years to come
A terrible odor of newly mown hay was floating in the air
But the others didn't hear a thing didn't feel a thing
Their crowd was a train blocked by a thousand whistle blasts
A train blocked by disembodied madness
A great mystery like a lost child
With those dirty tears seeking to imitate blood
And which are no more than oats
Close all the doors and windows
Let nobody out
Are the signals functioning
Where is that woman taking us
The madeporic coral pharmacy is crumbling
The woman spits on the injured man
Bushes of lovers throw their love flowers in the fire

Insubordination of previous sights

Luis Cernuda

Born and raised in Seville, Spain, Luis Cernuda (1902–63) obtained a law degree, but abandoned the legal profession in order to devote himself completely to poetry. In 1929, he moved to Madrid, where he participated in numerous literary and cultural activities. A member of the "Generation of '27," which included Federico García Lorca, Rafael Alberti, Vicente Aleixandre, and many others, Cernuda published three major collections of poetry in rapid succession. *Perfil del aire* (*Profile of the Wind*) (1927) was followed by *Un río, un amor* (*One River, One Love*), in 1929, and by *Los placeres prohibidos* (*Forbidden Pleasures*), in 1931. They were included five years later in his magnum opus, *La realidad y el deseo* (*Reality and Desire*). Greatly affected by the assassination of García Lorca in the Spanish Civil War, Cernuda abandoned Spain for England, France, the United States, and Mexico, where he finally died.

Nevada

En el Estado de Nevada
Los caminos de hierro tienen nombre de pájaro,
Son de nieve los campos
Y de nieve las horas.

Las noches transparentes
Abren luces soñadas
Sobre las aguas o tejados puros
Constelados de fiesta.

Las lágrimas sonríen,
La tristeza es de alas,
Y las alas, sabemos,
Dan amor inconstante.

Los árboles abrazan árboles,
Una canción besa otra canción;
Por los caminos de hierro
Pasa el dolor y la alegría.

Siempre hay nieve dormida
Sobre otra nieve, allá en Nevada.

Carne De Mar

Dentro de breves días será otoño en Virginia,
Cuando los cazadores, la mirada de lluvia,
Vuelven a su tierra nativa, el árbol que no olvida,
Corderos de apariencia terrible,
Dentro de breves días será otoño in Virginia.

Nevada

In the state of Nevada
The railroads are named for birds,
The fields are of snow
And the hours of snow.

The transparent nights
Project dream lights
Onto the waters or pure roof-tops
With their holiday constellations.

Tears smile,
Sadness sprouts wings,
And wings, we know,
Bring only fickle love.

Trees embrace trees,
A song kisses another song;
Sadness and happiness
Ride the railroad tracks.

There is always snow sleeping
On more snow, over there in Nevada.

Sea Flesh

In a few days autumn will arrive in Virginia,
When hunters, with looks of rain,
Return to their native land, the tree that never forgets,
Lambs terrible in appearance,
In a few days autumn will arrive in Virginia.

Sí, los cuerpos estrechamente enlazados,
Los labios en la llave más íntima,
¿Qué dirá él, hecho piel de naufragio
O dolor con la puerta cerrada,
Dolor frente a dolor,
Sin esperar amor tampoco?

El amor viene y va, mira;
El amor viene y va,
Sin dar limosna a nubes mutiladas,
Por vestidos harapos de tierra,
Y él no sabe, nunca sabrá más nada.

Ahora inútil pasar la mano sobre otoño.

Cuerpo En Pena

Lentamente el ahogado recorre sus dominios
Donde el silencio quita su apariencia a la vida.
Transparentes llanuras inmóviles le ofrecen
Árboles sin colores y pájaros callados.

Las sombras indecisas alargándose tiemblan,
Mas el viento no mueve sus alas irisadas;
Si el ahogado sacude sus lívidos recuerdos,
Halla un golpe de luz, la memoria del aire.

Un vidrio denso tiembla delante de las cosas,
Un vidrio que despierta formas color de olvido;
Olvidos de tristeza, de un amor, de la vida,
Ahogados como un cuerpo sin luz, sin aire, muerto.

Yes, bodies tightly entwined,
Lips in the most intimate key,
What will he say, made a shipwrecked hulk
Or pain with the door closed,
Pain confronting pain,
Without expecting love either?

Love comes and goes, look;
love comes and goes,
Without giving alms to mutilated clouds,
For clothing, earthen rags,
And he knows nothing else, and never will.

At present it is useless to caress autumn.

Body in Torment

Slowly the drowned man inspects his domains
Where silence effaces the appearance of life.
Transparent, motionless plains present
Colorless trees and silent birds.

Indecisive shadows tremble growing longer,
But the wind does not flap its iridescent wings;
If the drowned man shakes his livid memories,
He finds a flash of light, memories of air.

A sheet of glass trembles thickly before things,
A sheet of glass awakening forms the color of oblivion;
Forgotten sadness, love, life.
Drowned like a body with no light, no air, dead.

Delicados, con prisa, si insinúan apenas
Vagos revuelos grises, encendiendo en el agua
Reflejos de metal o aceros relucientes,
Y su rumbo acuchilla las simétricas olas.

Flores de luz tranquila despiertan a lo lejos,
Flores de luz quizá, o miradas tan bellas
Como pudo el ahogado soñarlas una noche,
Sin amor ni dolor, en su tumba infinita.

A su fulgor el agua seducida se aquieta,
Azulada sonrisa asomando en sus ondas.
Sonrisas, oh miradas alegres de los labios;
Miradas, oh sonrisas de la luz triumfante.

Desdobla sus espejos la prisión delicada;
Claridad sinuosa, errantes perspectivas.
Perspectivas que rompe con su dolor ya muerto
Ese pálido rostro que solemne aparece.

Su insomnio maquinal el ahogado pasea.
El silencio impasible sonríe en sus oídos.
Inestable vacío sin alba ni crepúsculo.
Monótona tristeza, emoción en ruinas.

En plena mar al fin, sin rumbo, a toda vela;
Hacia lo lejos, más, hacia la flor sin nombre.
Atravesar ligero como pájaro herido
Ese cristal confuso, esas luces extrañas.

Pálido entre las ondas cada vez más opacas
El ahogado ligero se pierde ciegamente
En el fondo nocturno como un astro apagodo.
Hacia lo lejos, sí, hacia el aire sin nombre.

Delicately, hastily, tremors begin to appear,
Vague and gray, igniting in the water
Reflections of metal or shining blades,
Whose course cleaves the symmetrical waves.

Tranquil flowers of light awaken in the distance,
Flowers of light, perhaps, or such lovely glances
As the drowned man was able to dream one night,
Loveless and painless, in his infinite tomb.

In their splendor the seductive water grows calm,
An azure smile appearing in its waves.
Smiles, oh the happy glances of lips;
Glances, oh smiles of triumphant light.

The delicate prison unfolds its mirrors;
Sinuous clarity, shifting scenes.
Scenes interrupted by that pallid face,
Its pain already dead, solemn in appearance.

Bearing his mechanical insomnia, the drowned man strolls.
The impassive silence smiles in his ears.
Unstable void with neither dawn nor dusk.
Monotonous sorrow, emotion in ruins.

Finally in the open, trackless sea, at full sail;
Toward the distance, further, toward the nameless flower.
Traversing as lightly as a wounded bird
That blurred crystal, those strange lights.

Pallid among the waves growing increasingly opaque,
The drowned man disappears blindly, lightly,
In the nocturnal depths like an extinguished star.
Toward the distance, yes, toward the nameless air.

Diré Cómo Nacisteis

Diré cómo nacisteis, placeres prohibidos,
Como nace un deseo sobre torres de espanto,
Amenazadores barrotes, hiel descolorida,
Noche petrificada a fuerza de puños,
Ante todos, incluso el más rebelde,
Apto solamente en la vida sin muros.

Corazas infranqueables, lanzas o puñales,
Todo es bueno si deforma un cuerpo;
Tu deseo es beber esas hojas lascivas
O dormir en ese agua acariciadora.
No importa;
Ya declaran tu espíritu impuro.

No importa la pureza, los dones que un destino
Levantó hacia las aves con manos imperecederas;
No importa la juventud, sueño más que hombre,
La sonrisa tan noble, playa de seda bajo la tempestad
De un régimen caído.

Placeres prohibidos, planetas terrenales,
Miembros de mármol con sabor de estío,
Jugo de esponjas abandonadas por el mar,
Flores de hierro, resonantes como el pecho de un hombre.

Soledades altivas, coronas derribadas,
Libertades memorables, manto de juventudes;
Quien insulta esos frutos, tinieblas en la lengua,
Es vil como un rey, como sombra de rey
Arrastrándose a los pies de la tierra
Para conseguir un trozo de vida.

I will tell how you were born

I will tell how you were born, forbidden pleasures,
As a desire is born above towers of fear,
Threatening bars, discolored bile,
Night petrified by fists,
Before everyone, including the determined rebel
Who disdains life within walls.

Impenetrable armor, lances or daggers,
Everything that deforms a body is good,
Your desire is to drink those lascivious leaves
Or to sleep in that soothing water.
It does not matter;
Already they pronounce your spirit impure.

Purity does not matter, the gifts that a destiny
Raised toward the birds with immortal hands;
Youth does not matter, a dream more than a man,
Such a noble smile, silken beach beneath the tempest
Of a fallen regime.

Forbidden pleasures, worldly planets,
Marble members that taste like summer,
Juice from sponges abandoned by the sea,
Iron flowers, as resonant as a man's chest.

Arrogant solitudes, demolished crowns,
Memorable liberties, cloak of youth;
Whoever insults these fruits, with darkness on his tongue,
Is as vile as a king, as a king's shadow
Groveling at the earth's feet
To obtain a morsel of life.

No sabía los límites impuestos,
Límites de metal o papel,
Ya que el azar le hizo abrir los ojos bajo una luz tan alta.
Adonde no llegan realidades vacías,
Leyes hediondas, códigos, ratas de paisajes derruidos.

Extender entonces la mano
Es hallar una montaña que prohibe,
Un bosque impenetrable que niega,
Un mar que traga adolescentes rebeldes.

Pero si la ira, el ultraje, el oprobio y la muerte,
Ávidos dientes sin carne todavía,
Amenazan abriendo sus torrentes,
De otro lado vosotros, placeres prohibidos,
Bronce de orgullo, blasfemia que nada precipita,
Tendéis en una mano el misterio,
Sabor que ninguna amargura corrompe,
Cielos, cielos relampagueantes que aniquilan.

Abajo, estatuas anónimas,
Sombras de sombras, miseria, preceptos de niebla;
Una chispa de aquellos placeres
Brilla en la hora vengativa.
Su fulgor puede destruir vuestro mundo.

He did not know the limits imposed,
Limits of metal or paper,
When chance opened his eyes beneath such a lofty light,
Where empty realities fail to reach,
Foul laws, codes, rats from ruined landscapes.

To extend one's hand
Is thus to find a forbidding mounttain,
An impenetrable forest that denies,
A sea that swallows youthful rebels.

But if anger, outrage, opprobium, and death
Eager teeth waiting to pierce your flesh
Unleash their threatening torrents,
Then you, forbidden pleasures,
Proud bronze, arbitrary blasphemy,
Hold the mystery in one hand,
A taste uncorrupted by bitterness,
Heavens, flashing heavens that annihilate.

Down, anonymous statues,
Shadows of shadows, misery, nebulous precepts;
A spark of those pleasures
Shines in the hour of vengeance.
Its splendor can destroy your world.

Telarañas Cuelgan De LA Razon

Telarañas cuelgan de la razón
En un paisaje de ceniza absorta;
Ha pasado el huracán de amor,
Ya ningún pájaro queda.

Tampoco ninguna hoja,
Todas van lejos, como gotas de agua
De un mar cuando se seca,
Cuando no hay ya lágrimas bastantes,
Porque alguien, cruel como un día de sol en primavera,
Con su sola presencia ha dividido en dos un cuerpo.

Ahora hace falta recoger los trozos de prudencia,
Aunque siempre nos falte alguno;
Recoger la vida vacía
Y caminar esperando que lentamente se llene,
Si es posible, otra vez, como antes,
De sueños desconocidos y deseos invisibles.

Tú nada sabes de ello,
Tú estás allá, cruel como el día;
El día, esa luz que abraza estrechamente un triste muro,
Un muro, ¿no comprendes?,
Un muro frente al cual estoy solo.

Cobwebs are Hanging from the mind

Cobwebs are hanging from the mind
In a landscape of astonished ash;
Love's hurricane has passed,
Not a single bird remains behind.

No leaves either,
They vanish like drops of water
In a sea that evaporates,
When there are not enough tears,
Because someone, cruel as a sunny day in spring,
Has cut a body in two by his simple presence.

Now one needs to gather bits of prudence,
Although one bit will always be missing;
To gather this empty life
And to continue on one's way hoping it will slowly fill,
If possible, once again, as before,
With unknown dreams and invisible desires.

You know nothing of that,
You are over there, cruel as the day,
The day, the light tightly embracing a wretched wall,
A wall, don't you understand?
A wall before which I find myself alone.

Unos Cuerpos Son Como Flores

Unos cuerpos son como flores,
Otros como puñales,
Otros como cintas de agua;
Pero todos, temprano o tarde,
Serán quemaduras que en otro cuerpo se agranden,
Convirtiendo por virtud del fuego a una piedra en un hombre.

Pero el hombre se agita en todas direcciones,
Sueña con libertades, compite con el viento,
Hasta que un día la quemadura se borra,
Volviendo a ser piedra en el camino de nadie.

Yo, que no soy piedra, sino camino
Que cruzan al pasar los pies desnudos,
Muero de amor por todos ellos;
Les doy mi cuerpo para que lo pisen,
Aunque les lleve a una ambición o a una nube,
in que ninguno comprenda
Que ambiciones o nubes
No valen un amor que se entrega.

Pasión Por Pasión

Pasión por pasión. Amor por amor.

Estaba en una calle de ceniza, limitada por vastos edificios de arena. Allí encontré al placer. Le miré: en sus ojos vacíos había dos relojes pequeños; uno marchaba en sentido contrario al otro. En la comisura de los labios sostenía una flor mordida. Sobre los hombros llevaba una capa en jirones.

Some Bodies Are Like Flowers

Some bodies are like flowers,
Others like daggers,
Others like ribbons of water,
But all of them, sooner or later,
Will be burns spreading across another body,
Using fire to transform a stone into a man.

But man sways in every direction,
Dreams of liberties, competes with the wind,
Until one day the burn heals,
And he becomes a stone again on a forgotten path.

I, who am not a stone, but a path
Trampled by bare feet passing by,
I am dying of love for all of them;
I give them my body to tread,
Whether it leads them to an ambition or a cloud,
Without anyone understanding
That ambitions and clouds
Are worth far less than love offered freely.

Passion for Passion

Passion for passion. Love for love.

I was in a street of ash, enclosed by vast buildings of sand. There I found pleasure. I looked at him: in his empty eyes were two little clocks; each was running in an opposite direction from the other. In the corner of his mouth he held a flower he had bitten off. On his shoulders he wore a cape torn to shreds.

A sus paso unas estrellas se apagaban, otras se encendían. Quise detenerle; mi brazo quedó inmóvil. Lloré, lloré tanto, que hubiera podido llenar sus órbitas vacías. Entonces amaneció.

Comprendí por qué llaman prudente a un hombre sin cabeza.

Nocturno Entre Las Musarañas

Cuerpo de piedra, cuerpo triste,
Entre lanas como muros de universo,
Idéntico a las razas cuando cumplen años,
A los más inocentes edificios,
A las más pudorosas cataratas,
Blancas como la noche, en tanto la montaña
Despedaza formas enloquecidas,
Desqedaza dolores como dedos,
Alegrías como uñas.

No saber donde ir, donde volver,
Buscando los vientos piadosos
Que destruyen las arrugas del mundo,
Que bendicen los deseos cortados a raíz
Antes de dar su flor,
Su flor grande como un niño.

Los labios quieren esa flor
Cuyo puño, besado por la noche,
Abre las puertas del olvido labio a labio.

When he passed some of the stars died out, others lit up. I tried to detain him, but I could not move my arms. I cried, I cried so much that I could have filled his empty sockets. Then dawn appeared.

I understood why a man is deemed prudent if he has no head.

Nocturne Among the Shrews

Body of stone, sorrowful body,
Between fleeces like the universe's walls,
Identical to the races during birthdays,
To the most innocent buildings,
To the most modest waterfalls,
White as night, while the mountain
Smashes insane shapes,
Smashes pains like fingers,
Joys like fingernails.

Not knowing where to go, where to return,
Seeking the compassionate winds
That wipe away the world's wrinkles,
That bless desires severed at the root
Before presenting their flower,
Their flower as large as a child.

Lips are seeking that flower
Whose fist, kissed by night,
opens the doors of oblivion lip by lip.

Aimé Césaire

Born and raised in Martinique, Aimé Césaire (1913–2008) won a prestigious scholarship to the Lycée Louis-le-Grand in Paris at the age of eighteen. In 1936, he began working on his long poem "Cahier d'un retour au pays natal" ("Notebook of a Return to the Native Land"), where the term *négritude* appeared for the first time. Described by André Breton as "le plus grand monument lyrique de ce temps" ("the greatest lyrical monument of our time"), the work was finally published three years later, in 1939. By this time Césaire had returned to Martinique, where he helped found the journal *Tropiques*. In 1941, he welcomed Breton and his wife, who were fleeing war-torn Europe and who would go on to spend the next four years in New York. Césaire was elected Mayor of Fort-de-France in 1945, and served as one of the island's deputies in the French National Assembly. Heavily involved in politics thereafter, he continued to write poetry and to publish books on a variety of subjects.

N'ayez Point Pitié

Fumez marais

les images rupestres de l'inconnu
vers moi détournent le silencieux crépuscule
de leur rire.

Fumez ô marais coeur d'oursin
les toiles mortes apaisées par des mains merveilleuses jaillissent
de la pulpe de mes yeux
Fumez fumez
l'obscurité fragile de ma voix craque de cités flamboyantes
et la pureté irrésistible de ma main appelle
de loin de très loin du patrimoine héréditaire
le zèle victorioux de l'acide dans la chair de la vie–marais–

telle une vipère née de la force blonde de l'éblouissement.

Soleil Serpent

Soleil serpent oeil fascinant mon oeil
et la mer pouilleuse d'îles craquant aux doigts des roses
lance-flamme et mon corps intact de foudroyé
l'eau exhausse les carcasses de lumière perdues dans le couloir
sans pompe
des tourbillons de glaçons auréolent le coeur fumant des
corbeaux
nos coeurs
c'est la voix des foudres apprivoisées tournant sur leurs gonds de
lézarde

Show no Mercy

Smoke away swamp

the prehistoric images of the unknown
turn toward me the silent dusk
of their laughter

Smoke away oh swamp oh sea-urchin heart
soothed by marvelous hands the dead stars spurt
from the pulp of my eyes
Smoke away smoke away
the fragile darkness of my voice crackles with flaming cities
and the irresistible purity of my hands summons
far far distant from my hereditary patrimony
the victorious zeal of acid in the flesh of life–swamp–

like a viper born from the blond force of a dazzling splendor.

Serpent Sun

Serpent sun eye fascinating my eye
and the sea lousy with islands crackling beneath the fingers
of the flame-thrower roses and my withered body still whole
the water raises the carcasses of light lost in the corridor without
ceremony
whirling icicles encircle the crows' steaming hearts
our hearts
the voice of the tamed thunderbolts turning on their crevice
hinges
transmission of lizards to the landscape of broken glasses

transmission d'anolis au paysage de verres cassés c'est
les fleurs vampires à la relève des orchidées
élixir du feu cental
feu juste feu manguier de nuit covert d'abeilles mon
désir un hasard de tigres surpris aux soufres mais l'éveil
stanneux se dore des gisements enfantins
et mon corps de galet mangeant poisson mangeant
colombes et sommeils
le sucre du mot Brésil au fond du marécage.

Phrase

Et pourquoi pas la haie de geysers les obéliques des heures le
cri lisse des nuages la mer en écart vert pâle fienté d'oieaux
vauriens et l'espérance roulant ses billes sur les faîtes et
entrefaîtes des maisons et les déchirures en dorades des
surgeons bananiers

dans les hautes branches du soleil sur le coeur heurté des matins
sur le tableau âcre du ciel un jour de craie de faucon de pluie
et d'acacia sur un portulan d'îles premières secouant leurs
cheveux de sel interjetés de doigts de mâts en toute main
à toute fin sous le battement de cil du hasard aux délices
chantées d'ombre un assassin vêtu d'étamines riches et calmes
comme un chant de vin dur

the vampire flowers relieving the orchids
elixir of the central fire
just fire mango tree fire covered with bees at night
my desire a chance of tigers surprised in the sulfurs but the
stannous
awakening gilds itself with the infantile strata
and my pebble body eating fish eating
doves and slumbers
the sugar of the word Brazil buried in the swamp.

Sentence

And why not the hedge of geysers the obelisk of the hours the clouds' smooth cry the sea to one side pale green shat upon by worthless birds and hope rolling its marbles on the houses' ridges and bridges and the dolphin rips of the banana tree suckers

in the sun's topmost branches on the morning's choppy heart on the sky's acrid painting a day of chalk of falcon of rain and of acacia on a chart-book of primeval islands shaking their salty hair interspersed with mast fingers in every hand to every end beneath chance's blinking eyelash with delights' singing shadow an assassin dressed in rich and calm muslins like a chant of hard wine

Prophétie

là où l'aventure garde les yeux clairs
là où les femmes rayonnent de langage
là où la mort est belle dans la main comme un oiseau saison de
   lait
là ou le souterrain cueille de sa porpre génuflexion un luxe de
   prunelles
plus violent que des chenilles
là où la merveille agile fait flèche et feu de tout bois

là où la nuit vigoureuse saigne une vitesse de purs végétaux

là où les abeilles des étoiles piquent le ciel d'une ruche plus
   ardente que la nuit
là où le bruit de mes talons remplit l'espace et lève à rebours la
   face du temps
là où l'arc-en-ciel de ma parole est chargé d'unir demain à l'espoir et
l'infant à la reine

            d'avoir injurié mes maîtres mordu les soldats du sultan
d'avoir gémi dans le désert
d'avoir crié vers mes gardiens
d'avoir supplié les chacals et les hyènes pasteurs de caravanes
je regarde
la fumée se précipite en cheval sauvage sur le devant de la scène
   ourle un instant la lave de sa fragile queue de paon puis se
   déchirant la chemise s'ouvre d'un coup la poitrine et je la
   regarde en îles britanniques en îlots en rochers déchiquetés se
   fondre peu à peu dans la mer lucide de l'air
   où baignent prophétiques
   ma gueule

                  ma révolte

                           mon nom.

Prophecy

there where adventure preserves its keen eyes
there where women radiate with language
there where death is lovely in one's hand like a milk season bird
there where the tunnel picks from its own genuflection abundant
plums
more violent than caterpillars

there where the graceful marvel employs every means to attain
its end

there where the vigorous night bleeds a speed of pure plants
there where the stars' bees sting the sky of a hive more ardent
than night
there where my heels' noise fills the space and raises time's face
backwards
there where the rainbow of my word will join with hope
tomorow and the royal heir with the queen,

for having cursed my masters bitten the sultan's soldiers
for having moaned in the desert
for having screamed at my guards
for having begged the jackals and hyenas caravan shepherds

I observe
the smoke rushes like a wild horse to the front of the stage hems
the lava with its fragile peacock tail an instant then ripping its
shirt suddenly opens its chest and I watch it dissolve little by
little into British isles into islets into jagged rocks in the air's
lucid sea
where my muzzle
my revolt
my name
bathe prophetically.

Mississippi

Hommes tant pis qui ne vous apercevez pas que mes yeux
    se souviennent
    de frondes et de drapeaux noirs
    qui assassinent à chaque battement de mes cils

Hommes tant pis qui ne voyez pas qui ne voyez rien
pas même la très belle signalisation de chemin de fer que
font sous mes paupières les disques rouges et noirs du
serpent-corail que ma munificence lave dans mes larmes

Hommes tant pis qui ne voyez pas qu'au fond du réticule
où le hasard a déposé nos yeux
il y a qui attend un buffle noyé jusqu'à la garde des yeux
du marécage

Hommes tant pis qui ne voyez pas que vous ne pouvez
m'empêcher de bâtir à sa suffisance
des îles à la tête d'oeuf de ciel flagrant
sous la férocité calme du géranium immense de notre soleil

Ton Portrait

je dis fleuve, corrosif
baiser d'entrailles,
fleuve, entaille, énorme étreinte
dans les moindres marais,
eau forcée forcenant aux vertelles
car avec les larmes neuves
je t'ai construite en fleuve

Mississippi

Men too bad you do not perceive that my eyes
  recall
  fronds and black flags
  committing murder at every blink of my eyelashes

Men too bad you don't see don't see anything
not even the gorgeous railroad signals
beneath my eyelids produced by the red and black discs of the
coral snake that my munificence bathes with my tears

Men too bad you don't see that at the handbag's bottom
where chance has placed our eyes
someone awaits a buffalo drowned to the hilt of the
swamp's eyes

Men too bad you don't see that you cannot
prevent me from building innumerable
islands with flagrant sky egg heads
beneath the calm ferocity of our sun's immense geranium

Your Portrait

I say river, corrosive
kiss of entrails,
river, gash, enormous embrace
in the minor marshes,
forced water foaming against the sandbars
for with new tears
I have made you a river

vénéneux
        saccadé
                triomphant
qui vers les rives en fleur de la mer
lance en balafre ma toute mancenillière

Je dis fleuve
comme qui dirait patient crocodile royal
prompt à sortir du rêve
fleuve
comme anaconda royal
l'inventeur du sursaut
fleuve
jet seul comme du fond du cauchemar
les montagnes les plus Pelées

Fleuve
à qui tout est permis
surtout emporte mes rives
élargis-moi
à ausculter oreille le nouveau coeur corallien des marées
et que tout l'horizon de plus en plus vaste
devant moi
et à partir de ton groin s'aventure
désormais
        remous
                et liquide

poisonous
        abrupt
                triumphant

which toward the sea's flowering shores
hurls its crab-apple course like a slash
I say river
as someone would say patient royal crocodile
prompt to emerge from dream
river
like a royal anaconda
the involuntary start's inventor
river
a single burst as within a nightmare
the epitome of volcanic mountains.

River
to whom everything is permitted
wash away my shores
expand me
to auscultate ear the tides' new coralline heart
and let the vaster and vaster horizon
before me
beginning with your snout venture forth
henceforth
        as a swirl
                and a liquid

René Char

René Char (1907–88) was born and raised in L'Isle-sur-Sorgue, a picturesque town situated in Provence. In August 1929, he sent a copy of his book, *Arsenal*, to Paul Eluard. Clearly intrigued, he came to see Char shortly thereafter. Inspired by this meeting, Char moved to Paris almost immediately to join the Surrealist movement. Closely involved with the Surrealists in the beginning, he contributed poems to their journals, and participated in various demonstrations. In addition, he became friends with a number of avant-garde painters, with whom he would later collaborate or write poems about. By the mid-1930s, however, Char had distanced himself from the Surrealists, with whom he remained on cordial terms. He returned to live in Provence. Continuing to write poetry both before and after World War II (1939–45), he served valiantly as a captain in the French Resistance.

Plissement

Qu'il était pur, mon frère, le prête-nom de ta faillite – j'entends tes sanglots, tes jurons – O vie transcrite du large sel maternel! L'homme aux dents de furet abreuvait son zénith dans la terre des caves, l'homme au teint de mouchard tuméfiait partout la beauté bien-aimée. Vieux sang voûté, mon gouverneur, nous avons guetté jusqu'à la terreur le dégel lunaire de la nausée. Nous nous sommes étourdis de patience sauvage; une lampe inconnue de nous, inaccessible à nous, à la pointe du monde, tenait éveillés le courage et le silence.

Vers ta frontière, ô vie humiliée, je marche maintenant au pas des certitudes, averti que la vérité ne précède pas obligatoirement l'action. Folle soeur de ma phrase, ma maîtresse scellée, je te sauve d'un hôtel de décombres.

Le sabre bubonique tombe des mains du Monstre au terme de l'exode du temps de s'exprimer.

Certitude

Sans lendemain sensible ni capitale à abréger.
Sans le péril sournois du chlore aux barrages qui abritent son île publique,
Ma réserve.
Sans cette lueur de talion qui perfore les meules hideuses où je me suis agité.
Sans ces forains tardifs aux bras chargés de lilas.
Sans ces perfections émaciées attirantes comme la rondeur classique.
Messager en sang dans l'émotion du piège, expiré le congé d'orage,
Je t'étreins sans élan sans passé, ô diluvienne amoureuse, indice adulte.

Crease

How pure my brother was, your failure's sponsor – I hear your sobs, your oaths – Oh life transcribed from the broad material salt! The man with ferret teeth irrigated his zenith in the caves' earth, the man with a spy's complexion caused adorable beauty to erupt in tumors everywhere. Old stooped blood, my governor, we watched the nausea's lunar thaw to the point of terror. We became dazed from our savage patience; an unknown, inaccessible lamp, at the world's tip accompanied the vigil of our courage and our silence.

Toward your frontier, oh humiliated life, I walk at present with certain steps, aware that truth does not necessarily precede action. Mad sister of my phrase, my sealed mistress, I will rescue you from your ruined mansion.

The bubonic saber falls from the Monster's hands following the time to express oneself's exodus.

Certainty

Without perceptible tomorrow nor capital to abridge.
Without the sly danger of chlorine at the dams shielding its
 public island,
My reserve.
Without equal retributions' gleam perforating the hidious
 millstones where
  I splashed.
Without these tardy fair-workers their arms laden with lilacs.
Without these emaciated perfections as pleasing as classical curves.
Bloody messenger in the trap's emotion, expired the storm's leave,
I embrace you without impulsion without a past, oh torrential
 lover, adult sign.

Le Loriot

3 septembre 1939

Le loriot entra dans la capitale de l'aube.
L'épée de son chant ferma le lit triste.
Tout à jamais prit fin.

Afin Qu'il n'y Soit Rien Changé

1

Tiens mes mains intendantes, gravis l'échelle noire, ô Dévouée;
la volupté des graines fume, les villes sont fer et causerie lointaine.

2

Notre désir retirait à la mer sa robe chaude avant de nager sur son coeur.

3

Dans la luzerne de ta voix tournois d'oiseaux chassent soucis de sécheresse.

4

Quand deviendront guides les sables balafrés issus des lents charrois
de la terre, le calme approchera de notre espace clos.

5

La quantité de fragments me déchire. Et debout se tient la torture.

6

Le ciel n'est plus aussi jaune, le soleil aussi bleu. L'étoile furtive de
la pluie s'annonce. Frère, silex fidèle, ton joug s'est fendu. L'entente
a jailli de tes épaules.

The Oriole

September 3, 1939

The oriole entered the capital of the dawn.
The sword of its song closed the sad bed.
Everything came to an end forever.

So Nothing may Change

1

Take my intendant hands, climb the black laldder, my Adoring Partner; the seeds' sensuality sends forth smoke, the towns are of iron and distant conversations.

2

Our desire removed the sea's warm dress before swimming on its heart.

3

In the clover of your voice tourneys of birds dispel any worry of drought.

4

When the sands scarred by the earth's slow chariots finally serve as guides, their calm will approach our private space.

5

The number of fragments lacerates me. And the torture stands erect.

6

The sky is no longer as yellow, the sun as blue. The rain's furtive star announces itself. Brother, faithful flint, your yoke has split. Understanding has spurted from your shoulders.

7

Beauté, je me porte à ta rencontre dans la solitude du froid. Ta
lampe
est rose, le vent brille. Le seuil du soir se creuse.

8

J'ai, captif, épousé le ralenti du lierre à l'assaut de la pierre
de l'éternité.

9

"Je t'aime," répète le vent à tout ce qu'il fait vivre.
Je t'aime, et tu vis en moi.

L'épi De Cristal Égrène Dans Les Herbes Sa Moisson Transparente

La ville n'était pas défaite. Dans la chambre devenue légère le donneur de liberté couvrait son amour de cet immense effort du corps, semblable à celui de la création d'un fluide par le jour. L'alchimie du désir rendait essential leur génie récent à l'univers de ce matin. Loin derrière eux leur mère ne les trahirait plus, leur mère si immobile. Maintenant ils précédaient le pays de leur avenir qui ne contenait encore que la flèche de leur bouche dont le chant venait de naître. Leur avidité rencontrait immédiatement son objet. Ils douaient d'omniprésence un temps qu'on n'interrogeait pas.

Il lui disait comment jadis dans des forêts persécutées il interpellait les animaux auxquels il apportait leur chance, son serment aux monts internés qui l'avait conduit à la reconnaissance de son exemplaire destin et quel boucher secret il avait dû vaincre pour acquérir à ses yeux la tolérance de son semblable.

Dans la chambre devenue légère et qui peu à peu développait les grands espaces du voyage, le donneur de liberté s'apprêtait à disparaître, à se confondre avec d'autres naissances, une nouvelle fois.

7

Beauty, I go to meet you in the cold solitude. Your lamp is rosy, the wind is shining. The evening's threshold is rising.

8

Captive, I have married the ivy's slow motion as it assaults eternity's stone.

9

"I love you," the wind repeats to all that it quickens.
I love you, and you live in me.

The Crystal Ear of Wheat Counts Its Transparent Harvest in the Grass

The town was not defeated. In the room grown lighter the bestower of liberty covered his love with an immense bodily effort, like that of the day's creation of a fluid. Desire's alchemy rendered their recent genius essential to the universe this morning. Left far behind their mother would no longer betray them, their mother who was so motionless. Now they preceded their future's country which so far contained only an arrow from their mouths that had just burst into song. Their eagerness encountered its goal immediately. They attributed omnipresence to a time when nobody asked any questions.

He told her how formerly he summoned the animals in the persecuted forests to present a priceless opportunity, his oath to the interned mountains which had led him to recognize his exemplary destiny and the secret mouth he had to conquer to acquire the tolerance of another like him.

In the room grown lighter that gradually acquired the vast spaces of a voyage, the bestower of liberty prepared to disappear, to mingle with other births, once again.

Marthe

Marthe que ces vieux murs ne peuvent pas s'approprier, fontaine où se mire ma monarchie solitaire, comment pourrais-je jamais vous oublier puisque je n'ai pas à me souvenir de vous: vous êtes le présent qui s'accumule. Nous nous unirons sans avoir à nous aborder, à nous prévoir comme deux pavots font en amour une anémone géante.

Je n'entrerai pas dans votre coeur pour limiter sa mémoire. Je ne retiendrai pas votre bouche pour l'empêcher de s'entrouvrir sur le bleu de l'air et la soif de partir. Je veux être pour vous la liberté et le vent de la vie qui passe le seuil de toujours avant que la nuit ne devienne introuvable.

Martha

Martha whom these old walls cannot appropriate, fountain mirroring my solitary monarchy, how could I ever forget you since nothing compels me to remember you: you are the present that accumulates second by second. We will unite without having to approach each other, to anticipate each other as two poppies making love form a giant anemone

I will not enter into your heart to restrict its memory. I will not retain your mouth to prevent it from opening onto the air's blueness and the thirst to depart. I want to be for you the freedom and the wind of life that crosses eternity's threshold before night disappears forever.

Malcolm De Chazal

Born on the island of Mauritius, where he lived for most of his life, Malcolm de Chazal (1902–81) worked as an agronomist on sugar plantations, and later for the Office of Telecommunications. Trained as an engineer, he was an accomplished poet and painter. In 1947, although unknown, de Chazal sent a copy of *Sens plastique* (*Plastic Sense*) to people he thought might appreciate it. At some point, it fell into the hands of the French Surrealists, who regarded its visionary aphorisms with total amazement. André Breton recognized the author's brilliance immediately, comparing him to the Comte de Lautréamont, who published *Les Chants de Maldoror* in 1869. Elsewhere, W. H. Auden called de Chazal "the most original French writer to emerge since the end of the Second World War."

Sens Magique (Excerpts)

II

L'eau dit à la vague:
"Tu me bois."
"Comment le pourrais-je?"
Reprit la vague,
"Je suis ta bouche."

C

Le vert
Passa la main
Sur l'épaule du jaune
Qui eut un frisson mauve.

CXLVII

La pierre
N'entend
Son coeur battre
Que dans la pluie.

CCLXXXIX

La branche
Prit
Ses jambes
A son cou
Et se sauva
dans la liane.

DVII

Le bruit
Se croqua

Magic Sense (Excerpts)

II

The water said to the wave:
"You are drinking me."
"How could I?"
Replied the wave,
"I am your mouth."

C

Green
Rested its hand
On yellow's shoulder
Which produced a mauve shudder.

CXLVII

The stone
Only hears
Its heart beat
In the rain.

CCLXXXIX

The branch
Took
To its
Heels
And escaped
Into the tropical creeper.

DVII

The noise
Munched itself

Et
Laissa
Ses dents
Dans les
Touches
Du piano.

DCLI
La carotte
Bouffait
La bouche
Du cheval
Qui lui
Mangeait
Le nez.

DCCXLIV
Les murs
Marchaient
A plat
Pour ne pas réveiller
La rue.

DCCL
L'auto
N'atteindra
Jamais
La vitesse
De la route.

And
Left
Its teeth
In the
Piano's
Keys.

DCLI

The carrot
Gobbled
The mouth
Of the horse
Which
Was eating
Its nose.

DCCXLIV

The walls
Were walking
Flat
So as not to wake up
The street.

DCCL

The car
Will never
Reach
The road's
Speed.

Robert Desnos

Born and raised in Paris, Robert Desnos (1900–45) joined the French Surrealists around 1922, and impressed them with his remarkable gifts. Able to fall into a hypnotic trance whenever he wished, Desnos spoke, wrote, and drew with amazing ease while asleep. Also adept at verbal acrobatics, he produced complicated wordplay with equal ease. Between 1920 and 1930, Desnos published more than eight books of poetry. Despite his brilliant beginnings, he failed to live up to his original promise, and was ejected from the Surrealist movement in 1930. Turning his back on his former friends, he resumed his journalistic activities, which the Surrealists had disapproved of, and turned to writing traditional poetry. During World War II, Desnos was an active member of the French Resistance. Arrested by the Gestapo in 1944, he was sent to several concentration camps, including Theresienstadt (in German-operated Czechoslavakia), where he died from typhoid fever.

Notre Paire Quiète …

Notre paire quiète, ô yeux!
que votre "non" soit sang (t'y fier?)
que votre araignée rie,
que votre vol honteux soit fête (au fait)
sur la terre (commotion).

Donnez-nous, aux joues réduites,
notre pain quotidien.
Part, donnez-nous, de nos oeufs foncés
comme nous part donnons
à ceux qui nous ont offensés.
Nounou laissez-nous succomber à la tentation
et d'aile ivrez-nous du mal.

Un Jour Qu'il Faisait Nuit

Il s'envola au fond de la rivière.
Les pierres en bois d'ébène les fils de fer en or et la croix sans branche.
Tout rien.
Je la hais d'amour comme tout un chacun.
Le mort respirait de grandes bouffées de vide.
Le compas traçait des carrés et des triangles à cinq côtés.
Après cela il descendit au grenier.
Les étoiles de midi resplendissaient.
Le chasseur revenait carnassière pleine de poissons sur la rive
au milieu de la Seine.
Un ver de terre marque le centre du cercle sur la circonférence.
En silence mes yeux prononcèrent un bruyant discours.

Our Feather who are tin …

Our feather who are tin, have fun!
Hollow be the eye, nay me.
The eye king done come,
the eye will be dumb.
On earth a shit is a sin, have one!

Give us this tray:
our deli be red.
And, fork, give us truss patches
ass we four give toes who
trust passes against us.
Lead a snot in to tempt Asians,
but the liver was from weasels.

One Day When it was Night

It flew off at the bottom of the river.
Stones of ebony iron wire of gold and a cross with no crossbar.
All nothing.
I hate her with love like every individual.
The dead man was breathing great gulps of emptiness.
The compass traced squares and triangles with five sides.
Then he descended to the attic.
The midday stars were shining brightly.
The hunter returned, his game-bag full of fish on the Seine's bank in mid-stream.
An earthworm marks the circle's center on its circumference.
Silently my eyes pronounced a resounding speech.

Alors nous avancions dans une allée déserte où se pressait la foule.
Quand la marche nous eut bien reposé nous eûmes le courage de
nous asseoir puis au réveil nos yeux se fermèrent et l'aube
versa sur nous les reservoirs de la nuit.
La pluie nous sécha.

Destinée Arbitraire

à Georges Malkine

Voici venir le temps des croisades.
Par la fenêtre fermée les oiseaux s'obstinent à parler
comme les poissons d'aquarium.
A la devanture d'une boutique
une jolie femme sourit.
bonheur tu n'es que cire à cacheter
et je passe tel un feu follet.
Un grand nombre de gardiens poursuivent
un inoffensif papillon échappé de l'asile.
Il devient sous mes mains pantalon de dentelle
et ta chair d'aigle.
ô mon rêve quand je vous caresse!
Demain on enterrera gratuitement
on ne s'enrhumera plus
on parlera le langage des fleurs
on s'éclairera de lumières inconnues à ce jour.
Mais aujourd'hui c'est aujourd'hui.
Je sens que mon commencement est proche
pareil aux blés de juin.
Gendarmes passez-moi les menottes.
Les statues se détournent sans obéir.

Next we advanced along a deserted path crowded with people.
When the walk had refreshed us we were brave enough to sit
down then upon awakening our eyes closed and dawn
drenched us with the reservoirs of night.
The rain dried us off.

Arbitrary Destiny

for Georges Malkine

Behold the time of the crusades
The birds persist in speaking through the closed window
like fish in an aquarium.
In a shop window
a pretty woman is smiling.
Happiness you are only sealing wax
and I pass by like a will-o'-the-wisp.
A great many guards pursue
an inoffensive butterfly escaped from the asylum.
In my hands it becomes a pair of lace panties
and your eagle's flesh
oh my dream when I caress you!
Tomorrow people will be buried free of charge
no one will ever catch a cold
we will speak the language of flowers
they will invent new kinds of lighting.
But today is today.
I sense that my beginning is near
like wheat in the month of June.
Handcuff me policeman.
The statues turn away without obeying.

J'ai Tant Rêvé De Toi

J'ai tant rêvé de toi que tu perds ta réalité.

Est-il encore temps d'atteindre ce corps vivant et de baiser sur cette bouche la naissance de la voix qui m'est chère?

J'ai tant rêvé de toi que mes bras habitués, en étreignant ton ombre, à se croiser sur ma poitrine ne se plieraient pas au contour de ton corps, peut-être.

Et que, devant l'apparence réelle de ce qui me hante et me gouverne depuis des jours et des années, je deviendrais une ombre sans doute.

O balances sentimentales.

J'ai tant rêvé de toi qu'il n'est plus temps sans doute que je m'éveille. Je dors debout, le corps exposé à toutes les apparences de la vie et de l'amour et toi, la seule qui compte aujourd'hui pour moi, je pourrais moins toucher ton front et tes lèvres que les premières lèvres et le premier front venus.

J'ai tant rêvé de toi, tant marché, parlé, couché avec ton fantôme qu'il ne me reste plus peut-être, et pourtant, qu'à être fantôme parmi les fantômes et plus ombre cent fois que l'ombre qui se promène et se promènera allégrement sur le cadran solaire de ta vie.

I have Dreamed of You So Often

I have dreamed of you so often that you are no longer real.

Is there still time to reach your vibrant body and to kiss on your mouth the birth of the voice that I adore?

I have dreamed of you so often that my arms, accustomed while hugging your shadow to cross my chest, would not yield perhaps to your body's contours.

That, before the actual apparition of what has haunted and governed me for days and years, I would probably become a shadow. Oh scales of love.

I have dreamed of you so often that there is probably no time left for me to awaken. I sleep on my feet, my body exposed to every appearance of life and love, and you, the only woman who counts for me today, I could touch a stranger's lips and forehead more easily than your own.

I have dreamed of you so often, however, so often walked, spoken, slept with your phantom that perhaps my sole recourse is to become a phantom among phantoms and a hundred times more shadow than the shadow that crosses and will joyfully cross the sundial of your life.

L'idée Fixe

Je t'apporte une petite algue qui se mêlait à l'écume de la mer et ce peigne Mais les cheveux sont mieux nattés que les nuages avec le vent avec les rougeurs célestes et tels avec des frémissements de vie et de sanglots qui se tordant parfois entre mes mains ils meurent avec les flots et les récifs du rivage en telle abondance qu'il faudra longtemps pour désespérer des parfums et de leur fuite avec le soir où ce peigne marque sans bouger les étoiles ensevelies dans leur rapide et soyeux cours traversé par mes doigts sollicitant encore à leur racine la caresse humide d'une mer plus dangereuse que celle où cette algue fut recueillie avec la mousse dispersée d'une tempête.
Une étoile qui meurt est pareille à tes lèvres.
Elles bleuissent comme le vin répandu sur la nappe.
Un instant passe avec la profondeur d'une mine.
L'anthracite se plaint sourdement et tombe en flocons sur la ville.
Qu'il fait froid dans l'impasse où je t'ai connue.
Un numéro oublié sur une maison en ruines
Le numéro 4 je crois.
Je te retrouverai avant quelques jours près de ce pot de
    reines-marguerites
Les mines ronflent sourdement
Les toits sont couverts d'anthracite.
Ce peigne dans tex cheveux semblables à la fin du monde
La fumée le vieil oiseau et le geai
Là sont finies les roses et les émeraudes
les pierres précieuses et les fleurs
La terre s'effrite et s'étoile avec le bruit d'un fer à repasser sur la
    nacre
Mais tes cheveux si bien nattés ont la forme d'une main.

The Obsession

I bring you this comb and a piece of seaweed that mingled with the sea's foam But your hair is braided better than the clouds with the wind with celestial blotches with quivering life and sobs so that twisting sometimes between my hands it dies with the waves and offshore reefs so abundantly that it takes a long time to despair of the perfumes and their flight with the evening when the comb steadfastly marks the stars buried in its rapid and silky course traversed by my fingers solliciting the sea's humid caress more dangerous than the tempest's scattered foam from which the seaweed was plucked
A dying star resembles your lips
They are turning blue like wine spilled on a tablecloth
An instant passes with the depth of a mine
Anthracite moans softly and rains down on the town in flakes
How cold it is in the cul-de-sac where we met
A number forgotten on a house in ruins
Number 4 I think
I will meet you in a few days by this pot of asters
The mines emit a muffled snore
The roofs are covered with anthracite
This comb in your hair like the end of the world
The smoke the old bird and the jay
The roses and the emeralds have finished blossoming
The precious stones and the flowers
The earth crumbles and radiates with the sound of someone
  ironing mother of pearl
But your carefully braided hair has the shape of a hand.

Vie D'ébène

Un calm effrayant marquera ce jour
Et l'ombre des réverbères et des avertisseurs d'incendie fatiguera
    la lumière
Tout se taira les plus silencieux et les plus bavards
Enfin mourront les nourrissons braillards
Les remorqueurs les locomotives le vent
Glissera en silence
On entendra la grande voix qui venant de loin passera sur la ville
On l'attendra longtemps
Puis vers le soleil de milord
Quand la poussière des pierres et l'absence de larmes composent
    sur les
grande places désertes la robe du soleil
Enfin on entendra venir la voix
Elle grondera longtemps aux portes
Elle passera sur la ville arrachant les drapeaux et brisant les vitres
On l'entendra
Quel silence avant elle mais plus grand encore le silence qu'elle
ne trouvera pas mais qu'elle accusera du délit de mort
prochaine qu'elle flétrira qu'elle dénoncera
O jours de malheurs et de joies
Le jour le jour prochain où la voix passera sur la ville
Une mouette fantomatique m'a dit qu'elle m'aimait autant que je
    l'aime
Que ce grand silence terrible était la grande révolte du monde
Et que la voix me serait favorable

Ebony Life

A frightening calm will mark this day
And the shadows cast by the streetlights and fire alarms will
exhaust the light
All will grow silent the quietest people and the most talkative
Finally squalling babies will die
Tugboats locomotives the wind
Gliding along silently
Coming from afar a great voice will pass over the town
We will wait a long time
Then toward my lordship's sun
When dust stones and the absence of tears fashion the sun's robe
on
the deserted public squares
We will finally hear the voice
It will grumble a long time before the gates
It will pass over the town snatching the flags and breaking the
windows
We will hear it
What silence before but an even greater silence that it will
leave undisturbed but will accuse of responsibility for the
approaching death that it will wither that it will denounce
Oh accursed and joyful day
The day the day soon when the voice will pass over the town
A ghostly seagull told me that it loved me as much as I loved it
That the terrible silence was my love
That the wind bearing the voice was the world's great revolt
And that the voice would look on me with favor.

Sous Les Saules

L'étrange oiseau dans la cage aux flammes
Je déclare que je suis le bûcheron de la forêt d'acier
que les martes et les loutres sont des jamais connues
l'étrange oiseau qui tord ses ailes et s'illumine
Un feu de Bengale inattendu a charmé ta parole
Quand je te quitte il rougit mes épaules et l'amour
Le quart d'heure vineux mieux vêtu qu'un décor lointain étire
ses bras débiles et fait craquer ses doigts d'albâtre
A la date voulue tout arrivera en transparence plus fameux que
la volière où les plumes se dispersent
Un arbre célèbre se dresse au-dessus du monde avec des pendus
et ses racines profondes vers la terre
C'est ce jour que je choisis
Un flamboyant poignard a tué l'étrange oiseau dans la cage de
flamme et la forêt d'acier vibre en sourdine illuminée par le
feu des mortes giroflées
Dans le taillis je t'ai cachée dans le taillis qui se proclame roi des
plaines.

Beneath the Willows

A strange bird in a flaming cage
I declare that I am a woodcutter in the steel forest
that the martens and otters are total strangers
a strange bird that twists its wings and lights up
An unexpected flare has bewitched your word
When I leave you it reddens my shoulders and love
The vinous quarter hour better dressed than a distant setting
stretches its feeble arms and cracks its alabaster knuckles
Everything will occur when it should with a more famous
transparency than the aviary where the feathers are scattered
A famous tree rises above the world with hanged men in its roots
penetrating deep into the earth
I have chosen this day
A blazing dagger has killed the strange bird in the flaming cage
and the steel forest vibrates silently illuminated by the dead
wallflowers' fire
In the copse I have hidden you in the copse that proclaims itself
king of the plains.

Paul Eluard

Born in Saint-Denis, on the outskirts of Paris, Paul Eluard (1895–1952) was a pseudonym adopted by Eugène Grindel when he began to write poetry. Together with André Breton, Louis Aragon, and Philippe Soupault, he founded the French Surrealist movement in 1924. Originally a member of Paris Dada, like most of his colleagues, he was a prolific poet who published more than seventy volumes of poetry during his lifetime. In addition to participating in numerous Surrealist activities, Eluard edited two journals: *Révolution Surréaliste* and *Surréalisme au Service de la Révolution*. In 1926, the publication of *Capitale de la douleur* (*Capital of Pain*) established his poetic reputation. Shortly before the outbreak of World War II, however, his interest in Surrealism waned. During the Nazi occupation of France, Eluard actively participated in the French Resistance. Denounced by the Germans for authoring *Poésie et Vérité* (*Poetry and Truth*) (1942), he and his wife were forced to move every month.

L'égalité Des Sexes

Tes yeux sont revenus d'un pays arbitraire
Où nul n'a jamais su ce que c'est qu'un regard
Ni connu la beauté des yeux, beauté des pierres,
Celle des gouttes d'eau, des perles en placards,

Des pierres nues et sans squelette, ô ma statue,
Le soleil aveuglant te tient lieu de miroir
Et s'il semble obéir aux puissances du soir
C'est que ta tête est close, ô statue abattue

Par mon amour et par mes ruses de sauvage.
Mon désir immobile est ton dernier soutien
Et je t'emporte sans bataille, ô mon image,
Rompue à ma faiblesse et prise dans mes liens.

Giorgio De Chirico

Un mur dénonce un autre mur
Et l'ombre me défend de mon ombre peureuse.
Ô tour de mon amour autour de mon amour,
Tous les murs filaient blanc autour de mon silence.

Toi, que défendais-tu? Ciel insensible et pur
Tremblant tu m'abritais. La lumière en relief
Sur le ciel qui n'est plus le miroir du soleil,
Les étoiles de jour parmi les feuilles vertes,

Le souvenir de ceux qui parlaient sans savoir,
Maîtres de ma faiblesse et je suis à leur place
Avec des yeux d'amour et des mains trop fidèles
Pour dépeupler un monde dont je suis absent.

The Equality of the Sexes

Your eyes have returned from an arbitrary land
That has never known a glance
Nor experienced the beauty of eyes, beauty of stones,
That of drops of water, of pearls in closets,

Of naked stones with no skeletons, oh my statue,
The blinding sun serves as your mirror,
And it seems to obey the powers of evening
Because your head is confined, oh statue overturned

By my love and by my primitive wiles.
My motionless desire is your final support,
and I carry you off peacefully, oh my image,
Inured to my frailty and caught in my net.

Giorgio De Chirico

One wall denounces another wall
And the shadows protect me from my frightened shadow.
Oh tower of my love towering over my love
The walls retreated blankly around my silence.

You, what were you protecting? Pure indifferent sky,
Trembling you sheltered me. The light outlined
Against the sky, once the sun's mirror,
The daylight stars among the green leaves,

The memory of others who spoke in ignorance,
Masters of my frailty, and I replace them
With loving eyes and all too faithful hands
Poised to depopulate a world where I am absent.

L'amoureuse

Elle est debout sur mes paupières
Et ses cheveux sont dans les miens,
Elle a la forme de mes mains,
Elle a la couleur de mes yeux,
Elle s'engloutit dans mon ombre
Comme une pierre sur le ciel.

Elle a toujours les yeux ouverts
Et ne me laisse pas dormir.
Ses rêves en pleine lumière
Font s'évaporer les soleils,
Me font rire, pleurer et rire,
Parler sans avoir rien dire.

Ne Plus Partager

Au soir de la folie, nu et clair,
L'espace entre les choses a la forme de mes paroles,
La forme des paroles d'un inconnu,
D'un vagabond qui dénoue la ceinture de sa gorge
Et qui prend les échos au lasso.

Entre des arbres et des barrières,
Entre des murs et des mâchoires,
Entre ce grand oiseau tremblant
Et la colline qui l'accable,
L'espace a la forme de mes regards.

Woman in Love

She is standing on my eyelids
And her hair is in my hair,
She has the shape of my hands,
She has the color of my eyes,
She is engulfed in my shadow
Like a stone against the sky.

She never closes her eyes
Nor lets me sleep.
Her dreams in broad daylight
Make the suns evaporate
Make me laugh, cry and laugh,
Speak when I have nothing to say.

Refusal to Share

In the evening of madness, naked and clear,
The space between objects has the shape of my words,
The shape of a stranger's words,
Of a vagabond who unties the sash around his neck
And who captures echos with this lasso.

Between the trees and the fences,
Between the walls and the jaws,
Between this great trembling bird
And the hill that overwhelms it,
Space is shaped by my gaze.

Mes yeux sont inutiles,
Le règne de la poussière est fini,
La chevelure de la route a mis son manteau rigide,
Elle ne fuit plus, je ne bouge plus,
Tous les ponts sont coupés, le ciel n'y passera plus,
Je peux bien n'y plus voir.
Le monde se détache de mon univers
Et, tout au sommet des batailles,
Quand la saison du sang se fane dans mon cerveau,
Je distingue le jour de cette clarté d'homme

Qui est la mienne,
Je distingue le vertige de la liberté,
La mort de l'ivresse,
Le sommeil du rêve,

Ô reflet sur moi-même ô mes reflets sanglants!

Sous La Menace Rouge …

Sous la menace rouge d'une épée, défaisant sa chevelure qui guide des baisers, qui montre à quel endroit le baiser se repose, elle rit. L'ennui, sur son épaule, s'est endormi. L'ennui ne s'ennuie qu'avec elle qui rit, la téméraire, et d'un rire insensé, d'un rire de fin du jour semant sous tous les ponts des soleils rouges, des lunes bleues, fleurs fanées d'un bouquet désenchanté. Elle est comme une grande voiture de blé et ses mains germent et nous tirent la langue. Les routes qu'elle traine derrière elle sont ses animaux domestiques et ses pas majestueux leur ferment les yeux.

My eyes are useless,
The dust's reign is finished,
The road's hair has put on its rigid coat,
It has ceased to flee, I have ceased to move,
All the bridges are cut, the sky will not pass over them again,
I am no longer able to see.
The world detaches itself from my universe
And, at the height of the battles,
When the blood's season fades in my brain,
I distinguish daylight from that human brightness

Which is mine,
I distinguish dizziness from freedom,
Death from intoxication,
Sleep from dreams,

Oh reflections on myself! Oh my bloody reflections!

Beneath the red Menace …

Beneath a sword's red menace, undoing the hair that guides some kisses, that points to where the kiss lies, she laughs. Boredom has fallen asleep on her shoulder. Boredom only grows bored with the laughing woman, the reckless woman, who has an insane laugh, an end of day laugh sowing beneath the bridges red suns, blue moons, faded flower from a disillusioned bouquet. She is like a great wheat wagon, and her hands send out tendrils and stick their tongue out at us. The roads she drags behind her are her pets, whose eyes close at her majestic steps.

Boire

Les bouches ont suivi le chemin sinueux
Du verre ardent, du verre d'astre
Et dans le puits d'une étincelle
Ont mangé le coeur du silence.

Plus un mélange n'est absurde
C'est ici que l'on voit le créateur de mots
Celui qui se détruit dans les fils qu'il engendre
Et qui nomme l'oubli de tous les noms du monde.

Quand le fond du verre est désert,
Quand le fond du verre est fané
Les bouches frappent sur le verre
Comme sur un mort.

Max Ernst

Dévoré par les plumes et soumis à la mer,
Il a laissé passer son ombre dans le vol
Des oiseaux de la liberté.
Il a laissé
La rampe à ceux qui tombent sous la pluie,
Il a laissé leur toit à tous ceux qui se vérifient.

Son corps était en ordre,
Le corps des autres est venu disperser
Cette ordonnance qu'il tenait
De la première empreinte de son sang sur terre.

Drinking

The mouths have followed the sinuous path
Of the ardent glass, of the starry glass
And in the well of a spark
Have consumed the silence's heart.

Mixtures are no longer absurd
One spies the creator of words
Who perishes in the net he engenders,
Who baptizes oblivion with all the world's names.

When the glass bottom is deserted
When the glass bottom is faded
The mouths knock on the glass
As if it were a corpse.

Max Ernst

Devoured by feathers and ruled by the sea,
He let his shadow become the flight
Of freedom's birds.
He left
The ramp to others stumbling in the rain,
He left their roof to others seeking validation.

His body was ready,
The others' body prepared to disperse
The order that he held
From his blood's first imprint on the ground.

Ses yeux sont dans un mur
Et son visage est leur lourde parure.
Un mensonge de plus du jour,
Une nuit de plus, il n'y a plus d'aveugles.

Au Hasard

Au hasard une épopée, mais bien finie maintenant.
Tous les actes sont prisonniers
D'esclaves à barbe d'ancêtre
Et les paroles coutumières
Ne valent que dans leur mémoire.

Au hasard tout ce qui brûle, tout ce qui ronge,
Tout ce qui use, tout ce qui mord, tout ce qui tue,
Mais ce qui brille tous les jours
C'est l'accord de l'homme et de l'or,
c'est un regard lié à la terre.

Au hasard une délivrance,
Au hasard l'étoile filante
Et l'éternel ciel de ma tête
S'ouvre plus large à son soleil,
A l'éternité du hasard.

His eyes peer from a wall
And his face adorns them clumsily.
Another daylight lie,
Another night; the blind have ceased to exist.

By Chance

By chance an epic poem, but now completely finished
Every act is the prisoner
Of slaves with ancestral beards
And the customary words
Are valid only in their memory.

By chance everything that burns, that gnaws
Everything that wears out, that bites, that kills
But what continues to shine
Is the agreement between man and gold,
Is a gaze linked to the earth.

By chance a deliverance,
By chance the shooting star,
And my head's eternal sky
Opens to embrace the sun
And the eternity of chance.

Dans La Brume ...

Dans la brume où des verres d'eau s'entrechoquent, où les serpents cherchent du lait, un monument de laine et de soie disparaît. C'est là que, la nuit dernière, apportant leur faiblesse, toutes les femmes entrèrent. Le monde n'était pas fait pour leurs promenades incessantes, pour leur démarche languissante, pour leur recherche de l'amour. Grand pays de bronze de la belle époque, par tes chemins en pente douce, l'inquétude a déserté.

Il faudra se passer des gestes plus doux que l'odeur, des yeux plus clairs que la puissance, il y aura des cris, des pleurs, des jurons et des grincements de dents.

Les hommes qui se coucheront ne seront plus désormais que les pères de l'oubli. A leurs pieds le désespoir aura la belle allure des victoires sans lendemain, des auréoles sous le beau ciel bleu dont nous étions parés.

Un jour, ils en seront las, un jour ils seront en colère, aiguilles de feu, masques de poix et de moutarde, et femme se lèvera, avec des mains dangereuses, avec des yeux de perdition, avec un corps dévasté, rayonnant à toute heure.

Et le soleil refleurira, comme le mimosa.

La Terre Est Bleue ...

La terre est bleue comme une orange
Jamais une erreur les mots ne mentent pas
Ils ne vous donnent plus à chanter
Au tour des baisers de s'entendre
Les fous et les amours

In the Mist …

In the mist where waterglasses collide, where snakes search for milk, a monument of wool and silk disappears. Here all the women entered last night bearing their frailty. The world wasn't made for their interminable strolls, for their langorous gait, for their quest for love. Anxiety deserted the turn of the century, that great bronze country, following its gently sloping paths.

We will have to do without gestures softer than fragrances, eyes brighter than power; there will be cries, tears, swearing, and gnashing of teeth.

Henceforth men who fall asleep will only be fathers of oblivion. At their feet despair will have the regal bearing of short-lived victories, of the halos that adorned us beneath the beautiful blue sky.

One day, they will grow tired of it, one day they will become angry, needles of fire, masks of pitch and mustard, and woman will arise with dangerous hands, with eyes of perdition, with a ravaged body, eternally radiant.

And the sun will flower anew, like the mimosa.

The Earth is Blue …

The earth is blue like an orange
No question of error words do not lie
They no longer serve as blackmail
It's the kisses' turn to conspire
Madmen and love affairs

Elle sa bouche d'alliance
Tous les secrets tous les sourires
Et quels vêtements d'indulgence
A la croire toute nue.

Les guêpes fleurissent vert
L'aube se passe autour du cou
Un collier de fenêtres
Des ailes couvrent les feuilles
Tu as toutes les joies solaires
Tout le soleil sur la terre
Sur les chemins de ta beauté.

Le Baiser

Un coq à la porte de l'aube
Un coq battant de cloche
Brise le temps nocturne sur des galets de prom

Un lancer de ramages
Entre deux transparences inégales
On ne va pas si tôt lever la tête
Vers la lumière qui s'assemble
Mais la baisser
Sur une bouche plus vorace qu'une murène
Sur une bouche qui se cache sous les paupières
Et qui bientôt se cachera derrière les yeux
Porteuse de rêves nouveaux
La plus douce des charrues
Inutile indispensable
Elle sait la place de chaque chose

She her wedding ring mouth
All the secrets all the smiles
And what garments of indulgence
To believe her stark naked.

The wasps blossom green
The dawn adorns her neck
With a necklace of windows
Wings cover the leaves
You have every solar joy
All the sun on earth
On the paths of your beauty.

The Kiss

A cock at dawn's door
A bell-clapper cock
Breaks the nocturnal time on prompt pebbles

A release of warbling
Between two unequal transparencies
Rather than raise one's head so early
Toward the gathering light
One lowers it
Upon a mouth more voracious than a moray eel
Upon a mouth concealed beneath her eyelids
That will soon hide behind her eyes
The bearer of new dreams
The sweetest of plows
Useless indispensable
It knows everything's place

Dans le silence
Collier rompu des mots rebelles
Une autre bouche pour litière
Compagne des herbes fiévreuses
Ennemie des pièges
Sauvage et bonne formée pour tous
Et pour personne
Bouche oublieuse du langage
Bouche clairée par les mirages de la nuit

Le premier pas sur cette route franche
Monotone comme un enfant
Mille orchidées à l'infini
Brillant brûlant pont vivant
Image écho reflet d'une naissance perpétuelle

C'est gagner un instant
Pour ne plus jamais douter de durer.

In the silence
A broken necklace of rebel words
Another mouth for a palanquin
The companion of feverish herbs
The enemy of snares
Savage and well formed for everyone
And for no one
A mouth forgetful of language
A mouth lit by the night's mirages

The first step on this deliberate path
Monotonous as a child
A thousand endless orchids
A shining burning living bridge
The image echo reflection of a perpetual birth

Is to gain an instant
To abolish all future doubt of enduring.

J. V. Foix

A prominent member of the Barcelona avant-garde, which included such luminaries as Joan Miró and Salvador Dalí, J. V. Foix (1893–1987) was an unusually fine poet. He helped to forge not only the Catalan response to French Surrealism, but also the modern Catalan idiom. The son of one of the best-known bakers in the city, Foix abandoned his legal studies to pursue a more exciting career in literature. During the 1920s, he edited and wrote for such journals as *L'Amic de les Arts* (*The Friend of the Arts*), which provided a forum for the Surrealist movement in Catalonia. Although Foix published numerous books of poetry, *Gertrudis (1927)* and *KRTU* (1932) best illustrate his Surrealist style. In 1981, he received the Gold Medal of the Government of Catalunya and, three years later, the Premi d'Honor de les Lletres catalanes for his contributions to Catalan culture.

Es Quan Dormo Que hi Veig Clar

A Joana Givanel

És quan plou que ballo sol
Vestit d'algues, or i escata,
Hi ha un pany de mar al revolt
I un tros de cel escarlata,
Un ocell fa un giravolt
I treu branques una mata,
El casalot del pirata
Es un ample gira-sol
Es quan plou que ballo sol
Vestit d'algues, or i escata.

És quan ric que em veig gepic:
Al bassal de sota l'era,
Em vestexio d'home antic
I empaito la masovera,
I entre pineda i garric
Planto la meva bandera;
Amb una agulla saquera
Mato el monstre que no dic.
Es quan ric que em veig gepic:
Al bassal de sota l'era.

És quan dormo qui hi veig clar
Foll d'una dolça metzina,
Amb perles a cada mà
Visc al cor d'una petxina,
Só la font ciel comellar
I el jaç de la salvatgina,

When I Sleep I see Clearly

For Joana Givanel

When it rains I dance alone
Dressed in seaweed, gold, and fishscales.
There is a stretch of sea on the horizon
And a patch of scarlet sky.
A bird turns a somersault overhead,
And a shrub sprouts branches.
The pirate's rambling mansion
Is a broad sunflower.
When it rains I dance alone
Dressed in seaweed, gold, and fishscales.

When I laugh I resemble a hunchback
In the pool beneath the threshing shed.
I dress like an old-fashioned gentleman
And pursue the farmer's wife,
And between the pines and the oaks
I plant my banner;
With a sack-maker's needle
I kill the unnamable monster.
When I laugh I resemble a hunchback
In the Pool beneath the threshing shed.

When I sleep I see clearly.
Crazed by a sweet poison
With pearls in both hands
I dwell in a seashell's heart
I am the spring in the ravine
And the wild beast's bed

O la lluna que s'afina
En morir carena enllà.
És quan dormo que hi veig clar
Foll d'una dolça metzina.

Les Cases …

Per a Joan Miró

Les cases, de roure i de caoba, s'enfilaven turó amunt i formaven una piramide caprici d'un artifex ebenista. Aquell era el poble on, sota el signe d'Escorpió, sojornava Gertrudis. Eren tan drets els carters, que em creia, abans d'ésser al cim, defallir. De l'interior de les cases sortien rares músiques com d'un estoig de cigars harmònic. El cel, de pur cristall, es podia tocar amb les mans. Blava, vermella, verda o groga, cada casa ténia hissada la seva bandera. Si no ha gués anat carregat d'un feixuc bidó de vernís, inelegant, m'hauria estret més el nus de la corbata. Al capdamùnt del carrer més ample, al vèrtex mateix del turó, sota una cortina blau cel, scia, en un tron d'argent, Gertrudis. Totes vestides de blau cel també, les noies lliscaven, alades, amunt i avall dels carrers, i feien com si no em veiessin. Cenyien el cabell amb un llaç escocès i descobrien els portals i les finestres on vidrieres de fosques colors innombrables dona ven al carrer el recolliment de l'interior d'una catedral submergida a la claror de les rosasses. El grinyol del calçat em semblava un cor dolcíssim, i la meva ombra esporuguia l'ombra dels ocells presoners de l'ampla claraboia celeste. Quan em creia d'atènyer el cim, dec haver errat la passa: em trobava en el tebi passadís interminable d'un vaixell transatlàntic. M'han mancat forces per cridar i, en clourem la por els ulls, desplegada en ventall, una serie completa de cartes de joc em mostrava inimaginables paisatges desolats.

Or the waning moon
Dying beyond the crest
When I sleep I see clearly
Crazed by a sweet poison.

The Houses …

For Joan Miró

The oak and mahogany houses clustered together on the hillside to form a pyramid, the whim of a crafty cabinetmaker. This was the town where Gertrude lived, beneath the sign of Scorpio. The streets were so straight I thought I would collapse before reaching the top. Strange melodies emerged from the houses' interiors as from a harmonious cigar box. I could reach out and touch the crystal sky with my hands. Blue, red, green, or yellow, every house was flying a flag. If I hadn't been carrying a heavy, inelegant pail of varnish, I would have adjusted the knot in my necktie. At the end of the widest street, at the very top of the hill, Gertrude was sitting on a silver throne beneath a skyblue curtain. Dressed entirely in blue as well, winged girls were gliding up and down the streets who pretended to ignore me. Their hair secured with a plaid ribbon, they were opening doors and windows whose innumerable panes, tinted in somber colors, gave the street the secluded appearance of a cathedral's interior submerged in the glow of its rose windows. The squeaking of shoes seemed to me like sweet choirs, and my shadow frightened the shadows of the birds imprisoned in the wide celestial skylight. When I thought I had finally reached the top, I must have taken a wrong turn: I found myself in the warm, endless corridor of an oceanliner. I could not muster the strength to cry out, and, as fear closed my eyes, a deck of playing cards spread out before me in a fan, revealing unimaginable desolate landscapes.

La Vila

La meva vila és sobre una plataforma circular. Totes les cases donen per llurs portals a la plaça i, perpendiculars, els deu carrers sense sortida. Al mig de la plaça, alta de cent metres, s'alça una torre millenària sense cap obertura. Al cim oncia una bandera negra teixida d'estels retallats de paper d'argent. No sap hom de ningu que hagi anat més enllà de la plaça i tothom ignora què hi ha més enllà dels murs que tanquen els carrers. No cal dir corn de segle en segle augmenten les llegendes que fan més paorosa l'existència exterior. El cel del meu poble, com els gonfanons del Via Crucis, té de nit i de dia, immòbils, el sol, la lluna i els estels, pàllidament lluminosos.

En desvetllar-nos, tots els loves del poble muntern les bicicletes i, a grans tocs de botzina, desvetllern el veinat. Les noies treuen les cadires als portals i s'hi asseuen. Miren tendrament com, els joves fem les nostres curses al voltant de la plaça, i es cobreixen el pit de medalles perquè guanyi llur amic. Tots portem brodat al jersei amb fil de seda de colors, el nom de l'estimada. Acabades les curses deixem els bicicles recolzats a la torre i anem a seure a costat del nostre amor. Ens donem les mans, i aixi passern hores i hores. Les mares obren els balcons i hi estenen els domassos. En acostar-se l'hora del repès, en un angle de la plaça s'obre una trapa i enmig d'una fumerola d'encens surt el pare Fèlix. Porta tot de llibres sota un braç i es passa l'altra mà per la barbassa. I diu, un dia: Déu es dóna sempre tot. Mai no dóna un braç, o una galta, o una cania. Ni mai no dóna un braç a un altre braç, o una galta a una altra galta, ni una cama a una altra cama. I, un altre dia, diu: La nostra vila és un acte d'amor de Deu, i totes les coses són fillet de l'amor. Aleshores ens mirem llargament als ulls i estrenyern més les Mans amoroses.

Fra Fèlix, entre una nova fumerola d'encens, se'n torna pel cotilló, carregat amb les bicicletes. El cel, amb el sol, la lluna i els estels, es mou suaument com una bambolina.

The Town

My town is on a circular platform. The doors of all the houses open onto the central square, along with ten dead-end streets that are perpendicular to it. In the middle of the square, rising one hundred meters, stands a thousand year old tower without a single opening. A black flag flutters at its top sown with stars cut from tinfoil. No one is known to have ever penetrated beyond the square, and nobody knows what lies on the other side of the walls that enclose the streets. Naturally, various legends have accumulated over the centuries that paint an even more fearful picture of outside existence. Emitting a pale light, the sun, the moon, and the stars are immobilized in my town's sky day and night, and on the banners in the Via Crucis. All the young men ride bicycles and prevent the neighborhood from sleeping by honking their horns. The girls drag chairs to the doorways and sit there. They watch tenderly as we young men run races around the square, and they cover their chests with medals awarded to their boyfriends. We all wear jerseys with our girlfriends' names embroidered in silk thread of different colors. When the races are finished, we leave our bicycles leaning against the tower and go sit with our girlfriends. We spend hours and hours holding hands. The mothers open the balconies and hang out their linen.

As the hour to retire approaches, a trapdoor opens in a corner of the square, and Father Felix emerges in a cloud of incense. He carries a pile of books under one arm and caresses his thick beard with the other hand. And one day he said: "God always takes everything for himself. He never gives an arm, a cheek, or a leg. Neither does he give an arm to another arm, nor a cheek to another cheek, nor a leg to another leg." And another day he said: "Our town is an act of love committed by God, and all the things in it are daughters of love. Let us therefore gaze into each others' eyes at length and extend our loving hands more often."

Surrounded by a new cloud of incense, Brother Felix makes his way back through the cotillion loaded down with the bicycles. Together with the sun, the moon, and the stars, the sky sways gently like a theater curtain.

S'havia Posat . . .

S'havia posat, com quan d'infant anava a les processons, un vestit de llustrina rosa amb una escampadissa d'estels retallats de paper d'estany, perruca rossa cenyida amb una corona de roses naturals, xinelles blanques amb els monogrames de Jesús i Maria brodats amb fil d'or, i dues minses ales esgrogueïdes.

M'esperava, com sempre, al celobert, entre el safareig, del qual sobreeixia una roja sabonera, i un bell paisatge de bidons de llauna, esbotzats, i negres atuells d'ús indeterminat.

¿Per què li hauria dit, si m'hagués estat possible de reprendre la paraula

t'has posat un vestit tan llarg? No se't veu el tornassol dels genolls i, a l'envelat, no et podré amanyagar les cames.

¿Per què una sabonera tan espessa cobreix l'aigua del safareig? Els vaixells de paper no hi podran navegar i, ni removent-la amb totes les meves forces amb el picador de rentar la roba, no hi podrem simular un oceà agitat.

Em prengué per la mà i, silenciosament, em féu davallar per una escala d'esglaons desiguals. Dues estives de travesses de via fèrria formaven un passadís fresquívol que illuminaven irregularment diminutes bombetes enteranyinades. Com li agraïa tanta de sollicitud a mostrar-me els meus paisatges dilectes! Foradades a mig fer, murallats riberencs, galeries subterrànies amb arbredes d'eixades i picots gegantins, reraeixides on pengen mil cordes inútils. Més que els panorames alpestres o els cims pririnencs, més que l'ample buc o la cova i la caverna naturals, em plau el desendreç de tants d'estris inútils on el rovell seductor brilla com una rosada providencial sota la claror moradenca que la meva companya hi aparia.

She had put on …

She had put on, like a girl preparing for a procession, a pink lamé gown sprinkled with stars cut from tinfoil, a blond wig with a crown of real roses, white slippers bearing the monograms of Jesus and Mary embroidered in gold, and two slender yellowish wings.

As usual she was waiting for me in the central patio, between the tank where the clothes were washed, which was overlowing with red foam, and a lovely landscape of mangled tin cans and black containers of indeterminate use.

"Why," I would have asked her had I been able to speak, "have you put on such a long dress? The sunflower of your knees has disappeared from sight, and I won't be able to caress your legs.

"Why does such a thick foam cover the wash tank? No one will be able to sail paper boats, and even if I move the wash paddle with all my strength, we won't be able to imitate the ocean's waves."

She took me by the hand and, silently, led me down a staircase with uneven steps. Two railroad ties formed a cool path which was illuminated irregularly by tiny lightbulbs covered with spiderwebs. How pleased she was to exhibit such solicitude in showing me my favorite landscapes! Half-finished tunnels, riverside walls, subterranean galleries with clumps of gigantic hoes and pickaxes, rear patios where a thousand useless cords hang. More than Alpine panoramas or the peaks of the Pyrenees, more than broad depressions or natural coves and caverns, I like the disorder of so many useless tools whose seductive rust shines like a providential dew beneath the purplish light prepared by my companion.

"Why do men praise mountains, woods, rivers, and springs and hypocrites despise the labyrinths they achieve in their metallic projections?"

¿Per què lloen els homes les muntanyes, els boscs, els rius i les fontanes, i menyspreen, hipòcrites!, els laberints que en llurs projeccions metàlliques realitzen?

En ple monòleg interior no m'havia adonat que acabàvem d'arribar a la sortida d'un túnel que duia a una vasta explanada on els homes gosaven exterioritzar llur divina aversió a la natura tot estrafent-ne la desordenada espontaneïtat amb figuracions tubulars de plom i d'argila. Uns altres homes, infatigables, escampaven per terra cabassades de graciosos utensilis de ferreteria i, al fons de tot, quatre homes més es perdien per la línia de l'horitzó, caregats cadascun d'ells amb una feixuga lletra diversa de l'alfabet, la lectura conjunta de les quals donava el nom misteriós: KURT, URKT, TRUK, UKRT, TURK, KRUT... del personatge central dels meus somnis.

Farem tard al ball hauria dit encara, si la paraula m'hagués respost al pensament.

La meva companya no era ja a costat meu. Reclosa per sempre dins el vehicle productor del generador trifàsic, vestida amb el seu vestit de ball fet de múltiples gases blau cel, s'allunyava tot acomiadant-se'm amb el somriure de mil blanques margarides i sense plànyer-se de la dissort que la condemnava a un càrcer tan llòbreg.

Jo, acotat més que mai en terra, fet un pellingot enquitranat de borra, aplicava unes pinces de soldadura elèctrica a un suport metàllic i illuminava la desolada vall d'inefables clarors celestes.

Lost in an internal monologue, I had not noticed that we had arrived at a tunnel's exit leading to a vast esplanade where men dared to exhibit their divine aversion to nature by mocking its disorderly spontaneity with tubular shapes of lead and clay. Some other men were tirelessly scattering basketfuls of graceful metal utensils on the ground, and in the background four more men were disappearing on the horizon, each weighed down by a different letter of the alphabet which, taken together, spelled the mysterious name: KURT, URKT, TRUK, UKRT, TURK, KRUT... of the central figure in my dreams.

"We will be late for the ball," I would have observed if my words had corresponded to my thoughts.

My companion was no longer by my side. Enclosed forever within the three-phase generator's productive receptacle, dressed in a ball gown made of multiple sky-blue gauzes, she took leave of me with the smile of a thousand white daisies without lamenting the misfortune that condemned her to such a gloomy prison.

Bending closer and closer to the ground, transformed into a rag smeared with muck, I applied some electric welding pliers to a metal beam and illuminated the desolate pit with an indescribable celestial brightness.

Notes Sobre La Mar

1 La sorpresa fou quan en haver pogut retirar, després de molts d'esforços, els bastidors on hi havia pintats tot d'atributs marítims, descobrírem la cleda misteriosa dels cavalls negres que, en ésser nit, vaguen a milers i milers per la platja amb una estrella al front.

2 Ben lligat el nas de cartó, grotesc, em pasejava pel moll amb un imponent diccionari de sinònims sota el braç. El barquer, vulgues no vulgues, em féu navegar mar endins. Era un pastor anglicà, i em volia demonstrar com els miracles més bells s'han esdevingut a la mar. En adonars-se, però, del meu nas arbitrari, tingué la polidesa de calars-se el seu. Aleshores, emfàtic, em digué que només la vanitat dels homes fa que, en el viure humà, del nostre planeta en diguin la Terra, però que Déu i els sants en diuen en llur llenguatge etern, la Mar; que la terra era només en el nostre planeta un accident, un fenomen transitori. "Els homes, em deia, són la colomassa de la mar." La gran inconeguda dels homes era, per al meu barquer, una peixera esfèrica errant pels espais celestes per a esbargiment dels àngels.

3 La mar, aquell matí, era un sòlid rectangular incolor i transparent com el cristall. Damunt seu, projectant-se obliquament en llargues, immensurables ombres còniques i cilíndriques, s'hi sostenien rares i originals figures de celluloide. Els pescadors, refets de llur sorpresa, asseguraven que eren l'esquelet dels estels, expellits del fons de la mar en produir-se aquel fenomen.

4 De levita i copalta negre, enguantats de negre també, els tres cavallers gesticulaven còmicament davant la mar color de taronja. En topar-me, recularen admirats. Sorprès jo a la vegada, vaig preguntar-los amb emoció precipitada: ¿Vosaltres també per ací? I riguérem follament. Aleshores vaig a posare-me el vestit negre, el copalta, els guants, i a dibuixar-me amb carbó tres amples rugues al front. Riba enllà, recordàvem, amb gests teatrals i simètrics, l'altra mar taronja on un dia imprecisable ens haviem topat també tots quatre, identicament abillats, i en el qual, riba enllà, també a grans riallades, intentàvem de recordar a quin segle, davant el país de la mar taronja, havíem discutit una vegada tots quatre a quin planeta pertanyia la mar on una vegada ells tres i jo, tots de negre, i rient, ens esforçavem a recordar ...

Notes on The Sea

1 The surprise came when, having succeeded after many attempts in retrieving the scenery painted with maritime themes, we discovered the mysterious corral of the black horses which, whenever night falls, roam the beach by the thousands with a star on their foreheads.

2 With my cardboard nose fastened securely, I walked grotesquely along the pier carrying an enormous dictionary of synonyms under my arm. Whether I liked it or not, the boatman made me sail out to sea. He was an Anglican minister who wanted to show me that the greatest miracles took place at sea. Perceiving my arbitrary nose, however, he had the good manners to put on his own. Then he emphatically informed me that the only reason we call our planet Earth is from human vanity, but that God and the saints refer to it in their eternal language as Sea; that earth was simply an accident on our planet, a transitory phenomenon. "Human beings," he told me, "are pigeon droppings in the sea." The great human enigma, according to my boatman, was a spherical fishbowl wandering through celestial space for the angels' amusement.

3 The sea that morning was a rectanglar solid, as colorless and transparent as a crystal. Overhead, casting long, immeasurable conical and cylindrical shadows, hovered rare and original celluloid figures. Recovering from their surprise, the fishermen explained that the skeletons of stars expelled from the bottom of the sea produced this phenomenon.

4 Wearing black frockcoats and tophats, as well as black gloves, the three horsemen gesticulated comically before the orange sea. On encountering me, they recoiled in amazement. Surprised at their sight, I exclaimed with sudden emotion: "You here too?" And we burst into laughter. Then I hastened to adopt their black costume, including tophat and gloves, and to draw broad wrinkles on my forehead with a piece of charcoal. Riding along the shore, we recalled, with theatrical and symmetrical gestures, another orange sea where one fine day we had also encountered each other, in identical costumes, and where, riding along the shore with much laughter, we tried to recall in which century, by the side of the orange sea, the four of us had previously discussed which planet the sea belonged to where previously the three of them and I, dressed all in black and laughing, tried to recall...

Joan Miró

Em sorprengué que, en ple abril de 1928, la sortida del túnel de Sant Gervasi fos obstruïda per la presència d'una colla de dames vestides de verd, amb capell i sabates de la mateixa color i segons la moda de 1890. Em sorprengué també que cadascuna d'elles mostrés ostensiblement, tot contemplant-la amb gests indesxifrables, una litografia que reproduïa, en grandària natural, la Gioconda. (Monna Lisa! Monna Lisa! em cridava un inspector dels F. de C. No, la Gioconda! La Gioconda!, responia jo desesperadament. Estiguérem a punt d'arribar a les mans.)

Aquell inspector em semblà molt forçut. Portava un bigoti excessiu que reproduïa exactament els "bigotis" tipogràfics. (Us conec: a vós us vaig veure pintat, el 1918, a les parets de les Galeries Dalmau, carrer de la Portaferrissa. En Joaquim Folguera m'assegurà aleshores que éreu el marit

d'una dama vestida sempre de verd. Sou un impostor! No passeu d'ésser el marit de cadascuna d'aquestes dames que ja són 30, 38, 49, 97, 100... i us heu deixat un bigoti com el d'En Joan Miró. Ni sou inspector ni sou En Miró. Però, Déu meu, ¿i si fóssiu el pintor Miró, marit de cadascuna d'aquestes dames? Sou En Miró, és cert, En Joan Miró, el pintor Joan Miró. ¿Què tal, Miró, com esteu, perdoneu, i cadascuna de les vostres mullers; per què heu deixat créixer damunt la vostra faç, a tort i a través, tants de bigotis, per a multplicar-vos com a marit de cadascuna de les vostres mullers?)

El comboi, un dos-cotxes Sarrià, passà de llarg per darrere el túnel. Jo continuava tot sol el meu diàleg, quan em vaig adonar que En Miró seia al meu costat, adormit en un son etern. En intentar de desvetllar-lo, la seva testa desaparegué misteriosament per la finestra, en forma d'òvul fosforescent; del tronc decapitat eixí un vol d'ocells en columna, i damunt la meva falda caigué una mà enorme, gelatinosa, com una materialització mediúmica de la mà de M. A. Cassanyes.

Quan em cria d'haver arribat a l'estació provisional de la Ronda, vaig constatar la presència de milers d'òvuls fosforescents que ascendien i descendien al llarg de la ribera d'una mar incògnita, i que flotaven inquiets per l'atmosfera. Anava a exclafar-ne alguns entre les meves mans i donar naixença als bells mons inèdits que porten en germen, si els meus braços no haguessin estat les branques caigudes d'una soca morta, que projectava damunt el paisatge una ombra escanyada.

Joan Miró

I was surprised to discover, in mid April 1928, that the outlet of the Sant Gervasi tunnel was obstructed by the presence of a group of ladies dressed in green, with matching hats and shoes, in the style of the 1890s. I was also surprised that each of them displayed a life-sized lithograph of *La Gioconda* which they contemplated with undecipherable gestures. ("*Mona Lisa*! *Mona Lisa*!," objected a municipal railway inspector. "No, *La Gioconda*! *La Gioconda*!," I replied desperately. We nearly came to blows.)

The inspector looked like a pretty tough customer. He wore an excessive mustache that closely resembled typographical "mustaches." ("I know you: in 1918 I saw your portrait on the Dalmau Gallery's walls, on Portaferrissa Street. Joaquim Folguera assured me at the time that you were the husband of a woman who always dressed in green. You are an imposter. You cannot be each of these ladies' husband they already number 30, 38, 49, 97, 100 ... and you have grown a mustache like Joan Miró's. You are neither an inspector nor Mr. Miró. However, my God!, suppose you were the painter Miró and were married to each of these ladies? But Mr. Miró shaved off his mustache some time ago. If you weren't wearing that mustache, I would say you were Mr. Miró. You are wearing neither an 1898 style mustache nor a mustache in the style of 1928; you are not clean shaven, inspector; you are not each of these ladies' husband. You are Mr. Miró, that's for sure, Mr. Joan Miró, the painter Joan Miró. How are you, Miró? How are you doing? Please excuse me, and each of your wives as well; why have you grown so many mustaches all over your face, for no apparent reason? In order to make a copy of yourself for each of your wives?)

Composed of two cars, the Sarrià train passed on the other side of the tunnel without stopping. I continued my dialogue by myself when I perceived that Mr. Miró was sitting beside me, asleep in an eternal dream. While I was trying to awaken him, his head disappeared mysteriously through the window in the form of a phosphorescent ovule; from the decapitated trunk issued a flight of birds in a column, and an enormous gelatinous hand fell into my lap, like the mediumistic materialization of M. A. Cassanyes' hand.

When I thought I had arrived at the temporary La Ronda station, I observed thousands of phosphorescent ovules ascending and descending along the shores of an unknown sea and floating restlessly in the atmosphere. I was about to crush some between my hands and release the beautiful unpublished worlds whose seeds they bear, if my arms had not been the fallen branches of a dead stump projecting a strangled shadow on the landscape.

Federico García Lorca

Born in Fuentevaqueros, near Granada, Spain, Federico García Lorca (1898–1936) was one of the most important Spanish poets and dramatists of the twentieth century. Like many of his Surrealist colleagues, he abandoned the study of law to devote himself completely to literature. In 1919, García Lorca traveled to Madrid, where he remained for the next fifteen years. At the Residencia de Estudiantes, he met other representatives of the "Generation of '27," including Rafael Alberti, Luis Buñuel, and Salvador Dalí, who introduced him to Surrealism. In contrast to his folkloric poetry, his flamenco compositions, and his gypsy ballads, García Lorca's hallucinatory verses of *Poeta en Nueva York* (1929) were dictated by a Surrealist muse. Written during a summer spent at Columbia University, New York, they translate his personal anguish into unforgettable urban images. Seven years later, during the Spanish Civil War, García Lorca was executed in Granada by Falangist militiamen, and his books were burned in the Plaza del Carmen.

La Aurora

La aurora de Nueva York tiene
cuatro columnas de cieno
y un huracán de negras palomas
que chapotean las aguas podridas.

La aurora de Nueva York gime
por las inmensas escaleras
buscando entre les aristas
nardos de angustia dibujada.

La aurora llega y nadie la recibe en su boca
porque allí no hay mañana ni esperanza posible;
a veces las monedas en enjambres furiosos
taladran y devoran abandonados niños.

Los primeros que salen comprenden con sus huesos
que no habrá paraíso ni amores deshojados:
saben que van al cieno de números y leyes,
a los juegos sin arte, a sudores sin fruto.

La luz es seputada por cadenas y ruidos
en impúdico reto de ciencia sin raíces.
Por los barrios hay gentes que vacilan insomnes
como recién salidas de un naufragio de sangre.

Dawn

Dawn in New York has
four pillars of muck
and a hurricane of black pigeons
splashing in the putrid waters.

Dawn in New York moans
on the immense staircases
searching between the corners
for spikenards of depicted anguish.

Dawn arrives and no one receives it in his mouth
because neither morning nor hope are possible:
at times furiously swarming coins
perforate and devour abandoned children.

The first to arise know in their bones
there will be neither paradise nor leafless loves:
they know the muck of numbers and laws awaits them,
of simple-minded games, of fruitless labor.

The light is buried by chains and noises
in a shameless challenge to rootless science.
Insomniacs stagger around in each district
like refugees from a shipwreck of blood.

Norma Y Paraíso De Los Negros

Odian la sombra del pájaro
sobre el pleamar de la blanca mejilla
y el conflicto de luz y viento
en el salón de la nieve fría.

Odian la flecha sin cuerpo,
el pañuelo exacto de la despedida,
la aguja que mantiene presión y rosa
en el gramíneo rubor de la sonrisa.

Aman el azul deserto,
las vacilantes expresiones bovinas,
la mentirosa luna de los polos,
la danza curva del agua en la orilla.

Con la ciencia del tronco y el rastro
llenan de nervios luminosos la arcilla
y patinan lúbricos por aguas y arenas
gustando la amarga frescura de su milenaria saliva.

Es por el azul crujiente,
azul sin un gusano ni una huella dormida,
donde los huevos de avestruz quedan eternos
y deambulan intactas las lluvias bailarinas.

Es por el azul sin historia,
azul de una noche sin temor de día,
azul donde el desnudo del viento va quebrando
los camellos sonámbulos de la nubes vacías.

Es allí donde sueñan los torsos bajo la gula de la hierba.
Allí los corales empapan la desesperación de la tinta,
los durmientes borran sus perfiles bajo la madeja de la caracoles
y queda el hueco de la danza sobre las últimas cenizas.

Negro Standards and Paradise

They hate the bird's shadow
on the white cheek's high tide
and the conflict of light and wind
in the hall of the freezing snow.

They hate the disembodied arrow,
the precise hankerchief of farewell,
the needle exerting rosy pressure
on the smile's blushing grass.

They love the deserted blue,
the swaying bovine expressions,
the deceitful moon of both poles,
the water's curved dance on the shore.

With the science of tree-trunks and rakes
they shower the clay with luminous nerves
and skate lubriciously over water and sand
tasting the bitter freshness of their millenary saliva.

It is in the crisp blue,
blue with neither a worm nor a sleeping footprint,
where the ostrich eggs rest eternally
and the dancing rains saunter about intact.

It is in the blue without history,
blue of a night with no fear of day,
blue where the wind's nakedness distorts
the empty clouds' sleepwalking camels.

There the torsos dream beneath the gluttonous grass.
There the corals soak up the ink's desperation,
the sleepers erase their outlines beneath the bundle of snails,
and the dance floor hovers above the final ashes.

Paisaje De La Multitud Que Vomita (Anochecer de Coney Island)

La mujer gorda venía delante
arrancando las raíces y mojando el pergamino de los tambores.
La mujer gorda,
que vuelve del revés los pulpos agonizantes.
La mujer gorda, enemiga de la luna,
corría por las calles y los pisos deshabitados
y dejaba por los rincones pequeñas calaveras de paloma
y levantaba las furias de los banquetes de los siglos últimos
y llamaba al demonio del pan por las colinas del cielo barrido
y filtraba un ansia de luz en las circulaciones subterráneas.
Son los cementerios. Lo sé. Son los cementerios
y el dolor de las cocinas enterradas bajo la arena.
Son los muertos, los faisanes y las manzanas de otra hora
los que nos empujan en la garganta.

Llegaban los rumores de la selva del vómito
con las mujeres vacías, con niños de cera caliente,
con árboles fermentados y camareros incansables
que sirven platos de sal bajo las arpas de la saliva.
Sin remedio, hijo mío, ¡vomita! No hay remedio.
No es el vómito de los húsares sobre los pechos de la prostituta,
ni el vómito del gato que se tragó una rana por descuido.
Son los muertos que arañan con sus manos de tierra
las puertas de pedernal donde se pudren nublos y postres.

La mujer gorda venía delante
con las gentes de los barcos y de las tabernas y de los jardines.
El vómito agitaba delicadamente sus tambores

Landscape of the Vomiting Multitude (Evening at Coney Island)

The fat lady came first,
ripping out roots and moistening the drum-heads.
The fat lady,
who turns dying octopi inside out.
The fat lady, the moon's enemy,
ran through the streets and the vacant buildings
leaving tiny pigeon skulls in the corners,
summoning furies from the last centuries' banquets,
calling to the demon of bread in the sky's well-swept hills,
filtering a longing for light in the underground tunnels.
These are cemeteries, I realize, cemeteries
and the pain of kitchens buried beneath the sand.
These are the dead, pheasants, and apples from another time,
which they stuff down our throats.

Muffled sounds arrived from the jungle of vomit
with empty women, with children made of hot wax,
with fermented trees and tireless waiters
serving plates of salt beneath the salivating harps.
It's hopeless, my son, vomit! No solution.
It's not hussars' vomit on prostitutes' breasts,
nor the vomit of a cat that happened to swallow a frog.
These are the dead who claw with clay hands
on flint gates where clouds and pastries are rotting.

The fat lady came first
with people from the ships and the taverns and the gardens.
Vomit was gently shaking its drums

entre algunas niñas de sangre
que pedían protección a la luna.
¡Ay de mí! ¡Ay de mí! ¡Ay de mí!
Esta mirada mía fue mía, pero ya no es mía,
esta mirada que tiembla desnuda por el alcohol
y despide barcos increíbles
por las anémonas de los muelles.
Me defiendo con esta mirada
que mana de las ondas por donde el alba no se atreve,
yo, poeta sin brazos, perdido
entre la multitud que vomita,
sin caballo efusivo que corte
los espesos musgos de mis sienes.

Pero la mujer gorda seguía delante
y la gente buscaba las farmacias
donde el amargo trópico se fija.
Sólo cuando izaron la bandera y llegaron los primeros canes
la ciudad entera se agolpó en las barandillas del embarcadero.

Muerte

A Isidoro de Blas

¡Qué esfuerzo!
¡Qué esfuerzo del caballo
por ser perro!
¡Qué esfuerzo del perro por ser golondrina!
¡Qué esfuerzo de la golondrina por ser abeja!
¡Qué esfuerzo de la abeja por ser caballo!
Y el caballo,

among a few girls of blood
who were asking the moon for its protection.
Woe is me! Woe is me! Woe is me!
This look belonged to me but is no longer mine,
a naked look trembling in alcohol
that dispatches incredible boats
through the piers' anemones.
I defend myself with this look
flowing from the waves where dawn fears to venture,
I, poet without arms, lost
among the vomiting multitude,
lacking an effusive horse to trim
the thick moss from my temples.

But the fat lady kept on coming
and the people were searching for drugstores
where they could find the bitter tropics.
Not until they raised the flag and the first dogs arrived
did the whole city rush to the pier's railings.

Death

For Isidoro de Blas

How hard!
How hard the horse struggles
to become a dog!
How hard the dog struggles to become a swallow!
How hard the swallow struggles to become a bee!
How hard the bee struggles to become a horse!
And the horse,

¡que flecha aguda exprime de la rosa!,
¡que rosa gris levanta de su belfo!
Y la rosa,
¡que rebaño de luces y alaridos
ata en el vivo azúcar de su tronco!
Y el azúcar,
¡que puñalitos sueña en su vigilia!
Y los puñales diminutos,
¡que luna sin establos, qué desnudos,
piel eterna y rubor, andan buscando!
Y yo, por los aleros,
¡qué serafín de llamas busco y soy!
Pero el arco de yeso,
¡qué grande, qué invisible, qué diminuto,
sin esfuerzo!

Paisaje Con dos Tumbas Y Un Perro Asirio

Amigo,
levántate para que
oigas aullar
al perro asirio.
Las tres ninfas del cáncer han estado bailando,
hijo mío.
Trajeron unas montañas de lacre rojo
y unas sábanas duras donde estaba el cáncer dormido.
El caballo tenía un ojo en el cuello
y la luna estaba en un cielo tan frío
que tuvo que desgarrarse su monte de Venus
y ahogar en sangre y ceniza los cementerios antiguos.

what a sharp arrow it squeezes from the rose!
What a grey rose it raises from its thick lips!
And the rose,
what a flock of lights and cries
is bound up in the lively sugar of its trunk!
And the sugar,
what tiny daggers it dreams during its vigils!
And the little daggers,
what a moon without stables, what nudity,
what eternal blushing skin they are seeking!
And I, crossing the eaves,
what a blazing seraphim I search for and am!
But the plaster arch,
how grand, how invisible, how tiny,
without struggling at all!

Landscape with two Graves and an Assyrian Dog

Friend,
get up and listen
to the Assyrian dog howl.
Cancer's three nymphs have been dancing,
my son.
They brought mountains of red sealng wax
and rough sheets where cancer was sleeping.
The horse had an eye in its neck,
and the moon was in such a cold sky
that it had to tear its mound of Venus
and drown the ancient cemeteries in blood and ashes.

Amigo,
despierta, que los montes todavía no respiran
y las hierbas de mi corazón están en otro sitio.
No importa que estés lleno de agua de mar.
Yo amé mucho tiempo a un niño
que tenía una plumilla en la lengua
y vivimos cien años dentro de un cuchillo.
Despierta. Calla. Escucha. Incorporate un poco.
El aullido
es una larga lengua morada que deja
hormigas de espanto y licor de lirios.
Ya viene hacia la roca. ¡No alargues tus raíces!
Se acerca. Gime. No solloces en sueños, amigo.

¡Amigo!
Levántate para que oigas aullar
al perro asirio.

Grito Hacia Roma (Desde La Torre Del Chrysler Building)

Manzanas levemente heridas
por finos espadines de plata,
nubes rasgadas por una mano de coral
que lleva en el dorso una almendra de fuego,
peces de arsénico como tiburones,
tiburones como gotas de llanto para cegar una multitud,
rosas que hieren
y agujas instaladas en los caños de la sangre,
mundos enemigos y amores cubiertos de gusanos

Friend,
wake up, the mountains still do not breathe,
and my heart's grass lies somewhere else.
It makes no difference that you are full of sea water.
For a long time I loved a child
who wore a little feather on his tongue,
and we lived inside a knife for a hundred years.
Wake up. Be silent. Listen. Sit up a little.
The howl
is a long purple tongue that deposits
fearful ants and iris liquor.
Now, it's coming near the rock. Don't extend your roots!
It is drawing near, moaning. Friend, don't sob in your dreams.

Friend!
Get up and listen
to the Assyrian dog howl.

Cry to Rome (From the Tower of the Chrysler Building)

Apples wounded oh so slightly
by slender, silver swords,
clouds rent by a coral hand
bearing a blazing almond on its back,
arsenic fish like sharks,
sharks like teardrops blinding a multitude,
roses that wound
and needles installed in the pipes of blood,
enemy worlds and loves covered with worms

caerán sobre ti. Caerán sobre la gran cúpula
que unta de aceite las lenguas militares,
donde un hombre se orina en una deslumbrante paloma
y escupe carbón machacado
rodeado de miles de campanillas.

Porque ya no hay quien reparta el pan y el vino,
ni quien cultive hierbas en la boca del muerto,
ni quien abra los linos del reposo,
ni quien llore por las heridas de los elefantes.
No hay más que un millón de herreros
forjando cadenas para los niños que han de venir.
No hay más que un millón de carpinteros
que hacen ataúdes sin cruz.
No hay más que un gentío de lamentos
que se abren las ropas en espera de las balas.
El hombre que desprecia la paloma debía hablar,
debía gritar desnudo entre las columnas
y ponerse una inyección para adquirir la lepra
y llorar un llanto tan terrible
que disolviera sus anillos y sus teléfonos de diamante.

Pero el hombre vestido de blanco
ignora el misterio de la espiga,
ignora el gemido de la parturienta,
ignora que Cristo puede dar agua todavía,
ignora que la moneda quema el beso de prodigio
y da la sangre del cordero al pico idiota del faisán.

Los maestros enseñan a los niños
una luz maravillosa que viene del monte;
pero lo que llega es una reunión de cloacas

will fall on you. They will fall on the great dome
that anoints the military tongues with oil,
where a man urinates on a dazzling dove
and spits coal dust
surrounded by thousands of tiny bells.

For there is no one to distribute bread and wine,
or to cultivate grass in the dead man's mouth,
or to unfold the linen of repose,
or to cry over the elephants' wounds.
There are only a million blacksmiths
who forge chains for the chldren to come.
There are only a million carpenters
who make coffins without crosses.
There is a crowd of laments
that tear open their clothes and wait for the bullets.
The man who despises the dove should have spoken,
should have screamed naked between the pillars
and given himself an injection of leprosy
and shed such terrible tears
that his rings and his diamond telephones dissolved.
But the man dressed in white ignores the wheat's mystery,
ignores the screams of childbirth,
ignores that Christ can still find water,
ignores that money burns the prodigy's kiss
and gives the lamb's blood to the pheasants' stupid beaks.

The teachers teach the children about
a marvelous light coming from the mountain;
but what arrives is a junction of sewers
where cholera's dark nymphs are screaming.
Devotedly the teachers point out the enormous domes perfumed

donde gritan las oscuras ninfas del cólera.
Los maestros señalan con devoción las enormes cúpulas
    sahumadas;
pero debajo de las estatuas no hay amor,
no hay amor bajo los ojos de cristal definitivo.
El amor está en las carnes desgarradas por la sed,
en la choza diminuta que lucha con la inundación;
el amor está en los fosos donde luchan las sierpes del hambre,
en el triste mar que mece los cadáveres de las gaviotas
y en el oscurísimo beso punzante debajo de las almohadas.
Pero el viejo de las manos traslúcidas
dirá: Amor, amor, amor,
aclamado por millones de moribundos;
dirá: Amor, amor, amor,
entre el tisú estremecido de ternura;
dirá: Paz, paz, paz,
entre el tirite de cuchillos y melenas de dinamita;
dirá: Amor, amor, amor,
hasta que se le pongan de plata los labios.

Mientras tanto, mientras tanto, ¡ay!, mientras tanto,
los negros que sacan las escupideras,
los muchachos que tiemblan bajo el terror pálido de los directores,
las mujeres ahogadas en aceites minerales,
la muchedumbre de martillo, de violín o de nube,
ha de gritar aunque le estrellen los sesos en el muro,
ha de gritar frente a las cúpulas,
ha de gritar loca de fuego,
ha de gritar loca de nieve,
ha de gritar con la cabeza llena de excremento,
ha de gritar como todas las noches juntas,
hasta que las ciudades tiemblen como niñas

with incense;
but beneath the statues there is no love,
there is no love beneath the eyes of definitive crystal.
Love is in the flesh torn by thirst,
in the tiny hut struggling against the flood;
love is in the dens where the serpents of hunger quarrel,
in the sad sea rocking the seagulls' carcasses.
and in the darkest kiss stabbing beneath the pillows.
But the old man with translucent hands
will say: Love, love, love,
acclaimed by millions of dying souls;
he will say: Love, love, love,
among the gold lamé quivering with tenderness;
he will say: Peace, peace, peace,
among the shivering knives and dynamite manes;
he will say: Love, love, love.
until his lips are covered with silver.

Meanwhile, meanwhile, oh, meanwhile,
the Negros who remove the spittoons,
the boys who tremble beneath the directors' pallid terror,
the women drowned in mineral oil,
the crowd bearing hammers, violins, or clouds
will scream even if they dash their brains against the wall,
will scream in front of the domes,
will scream driven crazy by fire,
will scream driven crazy by snow,
will scream with their heads full of excrement,
will scream like all the nights together,
will scream with their ragged voices
until the cities tremble like girls

y rompan las prisiones del aceite y la música.
Porque queremos el pan nuestro de cada día,
flor de aliso y perenne ternura desgranada,
porque queremos que se cumpla la voluntad de la Tierra
que da sus frutos para todos.

Vals En Las Ramas

Cayó una hoja
y dos
y tres.
Por la luna nadaba un pez.
El agua duerme una hora
y el mar blanco duerme cien.
La dama
estaba muerta en la rama.
La monja
cantaba dentro de la toronja.
La niña
iba por el pino a la piña.
Y el pino
buscaba la plumilla del trino.
Pero el ruiseñor
lloraba sus heridas alrededor.
Y yo también
porque cayó una hoja
y dos
y tres.
Y una cabeza de cristal
Y una violín de papel.

and destroy the prisons of oil and music.
Because we insist on our daily bread,
alder blossom and perennially harvested tenderness,
because we insist that the Earth's will be done,
that everyone receive its fruits.

Waltz in the Branches

One leaf fell
and a second
and a third.
A fish swam through the moon.
The water sleeps for one hour,
and the white sea sleeps for a hundred.
The lady
was dead among the branches.
The nun
was singing inside the grapefruit.
The girl reached for a pinecone from the pine tree.
And the pine tree
looked for the tiny song's feather.
But the nightingale
complained of his wounds everywhere.
And I too
because a first leaf fell
and a second
and a third.
And a crystal head
and a paper violin.
And the snow could sleep with the world

Y la nieve podría con el mundo
si la nieve durmiera un mes,
y las ramas luchaban con el mundo,
una a una,
dos a dos
y tres a tres.
¡Oh duro marfil de carnes invisibles!
¡Oh golfo sin hormigas del amanecer!
Con el muuu de las ramas,
con el ay de las damas,
con el croo de las ranas
y el gloo amarillo de la miel.
Llegará un torso de sombra
coronado de laurel.
Será el cielo para el viento
duro como una pared
y las ramas desgajadas
se irán bailando con él.
Una a una
alrededor de la luna,
dos a dos
alrededor del sol,
y tres a tres
para que los marfiles se duerman bien.

if the snow slept for a month,
and the branches struggled with the world,
one by one,
two by two,
and three by three.
Oh, the hard ivory of invisible flesh!
Oh, the dawn's abyss without ants!
With the whoosh of the branches,
with the ohs of the ladies,
with the ribbet of the frogs
and the yellow glug of the honey.
A shadow's torso will arrive
crowned with laurel.
For the wind the sky will be
as hard as a wall,
and the fallen branches
will go dancing with it.
One by one
around the moon,
two by two
around the sun,
and three by three
so the pieces of ivory will sleep well.

José María Hinojosa

Born in Campillos, near Málaga, José María Hinojosa (1904–36) studied law first in Granada, and then in Madrid, where he participated in literary gatherings at the Café Gijón. Through Emilio Prados, he met other members of the "Generation of '27" at the Residencia de los Estudiantes. In 1925, Hinojosa traveled to Paris, where he encountered a number of Surrealist poets and painters. A Surrealist convert, he attempted to involve his companions in similar activities when he returned to Madrid. The first of the Spanish Surrealists, according to Luis Cernuda, Hinojosa authored six books of poetry during his brief life. *La Flor de California* (*The Flower of California*) (1928) was probably the most significant contribution to the diffusion of Surrealism in Spain. Entitled "Textos oníricos" ("Dream Texts"), the second half consists of a lengthy text that seems to be the product of automatic writing. In 1936, during the Spanish Civil War, Hinojosa, his father, and his brother were executed by Republican militiamen.

Texto Onírico no. 2

Envuelto en un rumor de olas atajo en mi cerebro todos los pensamientos que pretenden escaparse por la escotilla y mientras apoyo mi mano sobre el testuz de Napoleón cae rodando mi cabeza por las cataratas del Niágara. Jamás he pretendido ser un saltimbanqui para apoyar mi cuerpo sobre el dedo del corazón y aunque lo afirmasen todos los horóscopos yo podria negarlo aún con solo dar una pincelada de azul cobalto sobre la estatua de la Libertad. Siempre podría negarlo y la negación sería infinita convirtiéndose en un punto negro enorme, lo suficiente para eclipsar al Sol y con esto me bastaría para bañarme tranquilamente a la luz de la Luna sin que las aguas mojasen mi cuerpo envuelto en el original de "La epistola a los Corintios." Yo soy la epistola y náufrago entre almas desvencijadas de ateos comulgaré todas las mañanas con almendras amargas.

Yo soy la epistola, corintios, tomad y comed porque mi cuerpo va detrás de mi cabeza por las cataratas del Niágara y mi alma está entre vuestras almas hecha epistola. ¡Tomad y bebed agua del Niágara por que es sangre de me sangre! Vuestros disparos no me hieren porque mi cuerpo es blanco y se confunde con las nubes y con la cal; con la espuma y con la sal. La nieve no me sirve para ocultarme, mi cuerpo ensangrentado la teñiría de rojo y los corintios se verían defraudados al encontrar mi rastro. ¡Oh! si la gran negación se transformase en este pez que llevo en la mano quizás se escurriría de entre mis dedos y caería al mar para dar la vuelta al mundo a través de las aguas pero la negación está firmemente entrelazada a mis dedos y tendría que sumergirlos en azufre para dejarlos en libertad.

¡Tomad y comed! ¡Tomad y bebed! Que el dedo del corazón entrará a rosca en la cúspide de la pirámide Cheops y quedará mi

Oneiric Text no. 2

Enveloped in the sound of waves, I intercept all my thoughts trying to escape through the hatchway, and while I place my hand on Napoleon's forehead my head rolls over Niagara Falls. I have never claimed to be an acrobat in order to balance my body on my middle finger, and even though all the horoscopes agree, I could still deny it by simply dabbing some cobalt blue on the Statue of Liberty. I could always deny it, and this denial would be infinite, transforming itself into an enormous black dot, large enough to eclipse the Sun, and with this I could bathe myself quietly by the light of the moon without wetting my body wrapped in the original copy of the "Epistle to the Corinthians." I am the epistle and castaway; among atheists' dilapidated souls I will receive the sacrament every morning with bitter almonds.

I am the epistle, Corinthians, drink and eat because my body passes behind my head over Niagara Falls, and my soul is made epistle among your souls. Take and drink water from Niagara Falls because it is the blood of my blood! Your shots do not wound me because my body is white and blends with the clouds and with the lime; with the foam and with the salt. The snow does not serve to hide me, my blood-stained body would dye it red, and the Corinthians would see themselves defrauded on encountering my face. Oh, if the great denial were transformed into this fish that I am carrying in my hand, perhaps it would slip from my fingers and fall into the sea in order to give the world its change across the waters, but denial is firmly intertwined with my fingers, and I would have to submerge them in sulphur to free them.

Drink and eat! Drink and eat! My middle finger will trace a spiral on the summit of the Cheops pyramid, and my body will remain suspended in the air hoping for the resurrection of the

cuerpo flotando en el aire en espera de la resurreción de la carne y de la apertura de las primaveras y para ello no necesitaré la partida de nacimiento ni la bendición de Su Santidad.

Entonces, corintios, haciendo de mi cuerpo un arco y de mi alma una flecha me dispararé en las cuatro direcciones de los puntos cardinales y caerá sobre todo en globo terestre una capa de ceniza roja hecha con la cremación de mi carne.

Granadas De Fuego

Esta granada abierta que está entre nuestras manos
tiene dientes de sange y carne de ballena
y ahora conserva intacta su agria arquitectura
porque fué desertora de las últimas guerras.

Entre vallados negros de gemidos y olas
sus granos desgranados iluman la tierra
rompiendo oscuridades con su roja sonrisa
en el perfil agudo del agua sin conciencia.

Con sus ascuas de nieve calcina la alegría
sobre un piso de mármol de alguna ciudad eterna
para dejar desnudas verdades en pirámides
de tempestad y miedo ondear sus bandereas.

Esta granada abierta no es el fruto de un árbol
que se engendró en el vientre de mares y de selvas;
en su cáscara amarga tiene amplitud de cielo
y en sus entrañas pican las aves y las fieras.

flesh and of the beginning of spring, and in this case neither a birth certificate nor His Holiness' blessing will be necessary.

Thus, Corinthians, making my body into a bow and my soul into an arrow, I will shoot myself in the four cardinal directions, and a cloak of red ash left from my flesh's cremation will descend on the entire terrestrial globe.

Pomegranates of Fire

This open pomegranate we are holding in our hands
has teeth of blood and a whale's flesh,
and its tart architecture is preserved intact
because it was a deserter in the last war.

Between black fences of moans and waves
the pile of seeds illuminates the earth,
rending the darkness with its red smile
bearing the sharp profile of the unconscious water.

With its snowy embers it roasts happiness
on a marble surface in some eternal city
in order to let naked verities wave their flags
in pyramids of storm and fear.

This open pomegranate is not the fruit of a tree
begotten in the belly of seas and jungles;
it has ample sky in its bitter peel,
and birds and wild animals nibble its bowels.

Vinieron Aves Heridas

Un ave herida se aquietó en mi frente
viendo huir tus miradas
dispersas por los aires mudos
de membranas mohosas y preguntas inútiles.

Tu aliento recortaba sobre nubes
el corazón sangriento
que en otro tiempo se ocultó en mi carne
y tu aliento bañaba de rocío
las dos manos abiertas enredadas en humo
que quieren alcanzar, sin conseguirlo
con sus dedos de cieno
el ave herida aquietada en mi frente.

Si a tus ojos no vienen a bañarse
panteras en acecho
ni nos muestras en ellos hostías blancas
hojas de carne perderán los árboles
porque a mi frente
presas dentro del cráneo
han venido a posarse aves heridas.

Wounded Birds Appeared

A wounded bird grew calm in my head,
coming to escape your glances
dispersed in the quiet air currents
of moldy membranes and useless questions.

Above the clouds your breath severed
the bloody heart
formerly hidden in my flesh,
and your breath bathed with dew
your two open hands entangled in smoke
whose fingers of muck
strove unsuccessfully to reach
the calm wounded bird in my head.

If stalking panthers don't come to your eyes to bathe,
nor our tokens become white communion wafers in your
eyes,
the trees will lose leaves of flesh
because inside my head,
imprisoned inside my skull,
wounded birds have settled.

Cuando Las Abejas Abren Sus Alas

En el borde desnudo de todas las esquinas
se alzan enredaderas con tus cabellos rubios
donde anidan las aves de plumas más ligereas
que recorren los mares de tus sueños azules
posadas en el mástil de algún barco corsario.

En el campo las flores quieren ser todas blancas;
pero mi corazón ¿qué color dá a mi pecho
cuando nublan las alas le miel que nos alumbra?
En el campo las flores quieren ser todas blancas
igual que las esquinas de tus gestos más blancos.

Mis dos manos resbalan por el limo verdoso
del fondo de este lago donde imprimes tus huellas
cuando tus ojos flotan en las aguas inmóviles
y mis ojos conservan la última luz del día.

Sobre mi piel elástica florecen los almendros
y abren como las rosas las abejas sus alas.

When The Bees Open Their Wings

On every corner's naked edge
convolvulus vines climb with your blond hair
in which lightly feathered birds make their nests,
scouring the seas of your blue dreams,
perched on the mast of some pirate ship.

The flowers in the fields all want to be white;
but my heart, what color do you dye my chest
when wings cloud the honey that illuminates us?
The flowers in the fields all want to be white
like the corners of your whitest gestures.

My two hands slide over the greenish slime
on the lake bottom where you leave your footprints
when your eyes float in the still water
and my eyes preserve the last light of day.

The almond trees blossom on my elastic skin,
and the bees open their wings like rose petals.

Marianne van Hirtum

Marianne van Hirtum (1935–88) exemplifies the third phase of French Surrealism. Born in Namur, Belgium, she moved to Paris in 1952, and met André Breton four years later. She joined the Surrealist group in 1959. An active member, Hirtum participated in various Surrealist activities, and collaborated on Surrealist journals such as *BIEF*, *La Brèche* (*The Breach*), and *L'Archibras*. Her first book, *Poèmes pour les petits pauvres* (*Poems for Poor Children*), appeared in 1953, and was followed by eight more works, including *Les Insolites* (*Bizarre Creations*) (1956), *La Nuit mathématique* (*The Mathematical Night*) (1976), and *Le Papillon mental* (*The Mental Butterfly*) (1982). Besides writing poetry, Hirtum was also an accomplished artist who, in addition to having numerous solo shows, participated in a number of Surrealist exhibitions.

Tricide

J'ai tué mon père et ma mère avec une petite fourchette–avec une petite fourchette–les ayant pris pour des oiseaux le long des arbres. J'ai tué mes parents avec la pince à sucre du grand-père: la chère idole n'a pas dit un mot à qui je lance chaque matin un respectueux coup de chapeau. Le chat de ma voisine m'a pris sous sa garde. Il est venu s'asseoir à côté de moi me surveillant sans cesse–sa crinière en peau de lapin fameusement bien brossée par derrière, et ses yeux en oeufs de cigogne.

Je suis seul à présent et triste à mourir:

tout le travail abandonné: je pleure–appuyé au petit cercueil où dorment côte à côte:

mon père et ma mère que j'ai tués avec une petite fourchette le jour maudit de mes seize ans.

Tigres Charmants

Tigres charmants
qui allumez la belladone
bêtes fleuries de soies
écartez de nous le péril
qui est d'exister mal
en n'étant pas

votre regard doit y suffire
implorante bulle d'iris
yeux noirs dont votre robe est saturée

Tricide

I killed my father and mother with a little fork–with a little fork–having mistaken them for birds along the trees. I killed my parents with grandfather's sugar tongs: the beloved idol to whom I respectfully tip my hat each morning didn't utter a word. My neighbor's cat took me under her protection. He came and sat next to me without diminishing his vigilance–with his rabbit fur mane wonderfully well brushed in back, and his eyes made of stork eggs.

I am all alone now and deathly sad:

all the work abandoned: I am crying–leaning on the little coffin where they sleep side by side: my father and mother whom I killed with a little fork the awful day I turned sixteen.

Charming Tigers

Charming tigers
who ignite the belladona
beasts decorated with silks
save us from the risk
of existing badly
by not existing

your gaze should suffice
imploring iris bubble
black eyes saturating your robe

têtes désemparées
naviguant sur la mer des cages
de quels silex bleus de désirs
ne l'avez-vous payée
notre liberté d'être un homme

Chanson De L'ours

Elles ont écarté sans y parvenir
tout ce qu'elles ont pu
les cloches de la nuit
et l'ours est allé plus boiteux
qu'une arme sans yeux
La bouche a cherché place en son visage
et ne l'a pas trouvée
sur le dos il n'a plus
qu'une échelle de poils
c'est la chaîne éternelle de l'ours
qui monte et qui descend

Le secret de l'ours est admis
dans la musique de deux yeux limpides
C'est un cortège que je vois
un bruit rouge
comme s'il était de castagnettes

Avons pelé les cinq éternités
les planètes vertes
avons dépassé les pays en croix

Les routes au-dessus de la terre
sont-elles praticables à présent?

heads bobbing helplessly
on the cages' sea
with what blue flints of desire
have you not paid for
our freedom to be human

Song of the Bear

They eliminated wihtout success
everything they could
the night bells
and the bear became lamer
than a weapon with no eyes
The mouth looked for a place on his face
but didn't find one
on his back he has only
a hairy ladder
it is the bear's perpetual chain
ascending and descending

The bear's secret is admitted
in the music of two limpid eyes
It is a procession that I see
a red noise
like that of castanets

we've peeled the five eternities
the green planets
we've outdone the cruciform countries

Are the roads above the earth
passable at present?

Dans Ces Chambres …

Dans ces chambres
le miel matinal me pénetrera
car ce sont chambres de l'esprit
Me parvient cependant la douceur
d'hélice de tes cheveux blonds
Sous la vitre opaque je sais
danser des neiges:
aussitôt me découvre
bête à tout dire
Qu'elle s'approche la jeunesse des chiffonniers
qu'aurez-vous à me reprocher
pas de jaunes sortilèges et peu d'espoir:
j'écoute jouer les gondoles
aux cordes en saumure de vent
Me rêve une vie de mammouth
en feuilles plus dures
que les trois pierres de notre amour
Si tu n'as plus un mot à dire
viens partager ma solitude cylindrique
où petites filles nous ferons la ronde
Je peux bien refermer les mains
sur ton corps de femme:
sera la plus aimée ta tête de triangle
couchée entre les seins
Je suis la bête qui peut tout faire
ce matin

In These Rooms …

In these rooms
the morning honey penetrates me
for they are mental rooms
However your blond hair's spiral
sweetness reaches me
Beneath the opaque windowpane I know
snows are dancing:
suddenly I find-myself
totally speechless
Let the ragpickers' youth approach
what will you have to reproach me for
no yellow spells and little hope:
I listen to the gondolas playing
on strings of wind pickles
dream of a mammoth life
in leaves harder
than the three stones of our love
If you have nothing to add
come share my cylindrical solitude
where little girls will circle around us
I can certainly close my hands
on your woman's body:
lying between your breasts
your triangular head will receive the most love
I am an animal capable of anything
this morning

Aller Dans La Vigueur …

Aller dans la vigueur de la nuit
s'accrochant aux hampes des enfants-navires:
le cerne des yeux s'agrandit d'ombre blanche
alors que sans mesure sauvage
la bête aveugle pose sa tête au nord du lit.

Nous eûmes des vents clairs tout au long du voyage:
pas encore un seul qui en est revenu
à peine celui-ci au long regard de pervenche qui s'éventaille,
brille sur la main qui ne parle que bleu
ce regard qui prend à la Reine sans défaut.

Mais devenir les enfants du pire!
Alors que la grande porte du jamais permis
sur un signal du regard tendre
s'abat sur nos coeurs–ténébreuse et folle!

A Voyage in the Vigor …

A voyage in the vigor of night
clutching the ship-children's flanks:
white shadows expand the eyes' orbits
while lacking in primitive moderation
the blind beast rests its head to the bed's north.

We experienced clear winds throughout the trip:
not a single traveler has returned
save one with a periwinkle's lengthy gaze opening like a fan;
sparkling on the hand that utters nothing but blue
a gaze seizes the peerless Queen by the throat.

But to inherit the worst!
While the great door to forbidden realms
at a signal from the tender gaze
pounces on our hearts–sinister and insane.

Miguel Labordeta

Miguel Labordeta (1921–69) was born and raised in Zaragoza, Spain. After receiving a Master's degree in History from the University of Zaragoza, he traveled to Madrid with the intention of earning a doctorate, but succumbed to his love of poetry, writing instead. His first book of poems, *Sumido25* (*Sunken 25*) (1948), dates from this period. Returning to his native city, Labordeta set about developing his craft and honing his Surrealist style. Two volumes of poetry appeared in rapid succession: *Violento idílico* (*Idyllic Violence*), in 1949, and *Transeúnte central* (*Central Transient*), in 1950. As with Labordeta's later poetry, these works depict a meaningless world, characterized by indifference and solitude.

Matinal

Cuando los besos
saben a mojadas pálidas
de ojos oscuros de pájaro enlazado
con nacimientos de montañas
tras duro trance que agoniza
en las escafandras de barro
de las sumisas embarazadas sin nariz.

Cuando entre cristales descuajados
rompecabezas de cuadrumanos
henchidos de infancias terminales
surge Osiris el profesor estelar
abriendo de par en par
los costados de los jóvenes alumnos de la madrugada
cortando con navajas de afeitar
los dulces párpados cerrados
caminantes sin tregua
por sollozos de los niños de pecho.

Cuando en las ventanas de la casas
los sueños incestuosos dejan paso
a las modestas sustracciones de los sueldos
y el diluvio de las duchas
quema los secretos homicidas
de los desayunantes
mientras los indefensos ascensores
inician su agobiante jornada
de puñetazos y periódicos
entre aullidos roncos

Morning

When kisses
taste like pale, moist women
with dark bird eyes linked
to the birth of mountains
behind the difficult moment dying
in the earthenware diving suits
of the noseless, pregnant, submissive women.

When among liquified crystals,
primate puzzles
filled with terminal childhoods,
the stellar professor Osiris emerges,
slashing open
the flanks of young students of the dawn,
using razor blades to cut
their soft, closed eyelids,
ceaseless travelers
through sobs from the children of their chests.

When incestuous dreams yield
in the houses' windows
to the salaries' modest deductions
and the flooding showers
burning secret homicides
of those eating breakfast
while the defenseless elevators
begin their exhausting work day
of punches and newspapers
among the hoarse howls

de la tenue hierba alzada
de las alambradas de la noche
y corruptas mariposas sin piedad
arrastran por los asfaltos fosforescentes
las miradas confusas de los homosexuales.

Cuando las mujeres se trasladan sin horror
a la máscara audaz de los espejos
esperando juzgar la calavera por su rictus
y el hombre es un pánico abstracto
que busca entre muchedumbre de ojeras
el puro cumplimiento
ya marchito
de arcanas profecías desterradas
en la fiebre de armonía
que en el corazón de la ateas hormigas
yace vinculado con el mágico rumor
de las charcas podridas
donde serán hermosas ciudades aun sin nombre.

Entonces hermano mío
un nuevo día
un otro día
se posa sobre el mundo
y en el eje imaginario del mundo
los muertos cantan su maravilla perecedera.

of the tenuous, insolent grass,
of the night's barbed wire fences,
and corrupt, pitiless butterflies
drag the homosexuals' confused glances
over the phosphorescent asphalt.

When the women go without horror
to the mirrors' bold mask,
expecting to judge their skulls by their grins,
and man is an abstract panic
looking among the crowd of eye-baths
for the pure execution,
already faded away,
of arcane prophecies bannished
in the fever of harmony
attached to the magic sound
centered in the hearts of the atheist ants,
the sound of putrid ponds
where beautiful cities will arise without number.

Therefore my brother
a new day,
another day,
settles on the world
where, aligned along its imaginary axis,
the dead sing their ephemeral miracle.

Carlinga

VOMITO ciudades derretidas pavesas
acechando al brujo de los manómetros.

"Por las lejanías teléfonos color de rosa
una hermosa existente de cabellos antiguos preguntaba por ti."

ESCUPO sanguinarios bosques fusilados
por mi boca seca de canguro abortado,
donde cayó el crimen supremo de las victorias
con todo su espesor de muchedumbre triturada.

"¿No sabeis? ..., preguntaban por ti ...
una mirada cándida anhelaba tu nombre
en el viento dorado del estío
por las lejanías teléfonos color de rosa."

SUDO angustia y momento cadáver
por las configuraciones finitas del aliento
que exhalan los astros bombardeados
en la noche que asoma de las ciegas persianas
donde habitantes cetrinos se muerden impertérritos
roídos de tristeza y vianda amarga de nuca.

"Repetían tu nombre
si el mar era montaña o vaho
una graciosa palabra tierna
por las lejanías teléfonos color de rosa."

RUMIO fósforos de locura y periódico
destruído en los hangares ciegos,
donde cada pitillo incierto

Cockpit

I VOMIT melted cities, sparks
awaiting the manometer's sorcerer.

"On the pink long distance telephone
a lovely lady with ancient hair was asking for you."

I SPIT bloody forests shot to pieces
by my dry, aborted kangaroo mouth,
where the victories' supreme crime occurred
with the density of a pulverized crowd.

"Don't you know? ... They wanted to talk to you ...
a candid glance yearned for your name
in the golden wind of summer
on the pink long distance telephone."

I SWEAT anguish and cadaverous moments
through my face's finite configurations
that exhale the bombarded stars
in the night appearing through the Venetian blinds
where sallow inhabitants bite each other impassively,
gnawed by sorrow and bitter nape of neck food.

"They repeated your name
if the sea was a mountain or vapor,
a gracious, delicate word
on the pink long distance telephone."

I CHEW matches of madness and old
newspaper in the blind hangars,
where each wobbly cigarette

apuñala la esperanza de un tumba pequeñita,
en la que sólo quepan mar-tierra-cielo-fuego y estrellas,
pero no mi congoja ni mi asalto mortal
por detener los ríos de ira y cumbre terrible
que borbotan de mi ser de rabioso varón funesto
hacia el ocaso de una temblorosa fuente amenazada
que furiosamente golpeo
con mi puño a mil kilómetros por hora.

"Te llamaban ...
¿Está?, preguntaban;
nosotros reíamos tu aventura inaudita,
pero la voz dulce se quebraba en sollozos
por las lejanías teléfono color de rosa."

SUEÑO que quizá llegue a existir,
pero las dos de la madrugada blanca
es una patrulla durísima de cascos implacables
sobre sucias colchonetas de agosto
que golpean la sien solitaria en formación
de las urbes hambrientas de destino.

"No está ...,
no está ..., dijimos,
y aquel hilo denso se rasgó en opaca sordera
y un invierno al galope se abalanzó dolido
por las lejanías teléfonos color de rosa."

SILENCIO mi profundidad de ruina
y en mi caverna el grito se corroe vitriolo,
por eso mis tubos pulmonares
no son sino ratitas putrefactas
y mi esperanza honda de suicidio
un ardiente colapso.

stabs the hope of a tiny tomb
barely enclosing sea-land-sky-fire and stars,
but not my anguish nor my mortal attempt
to restrain the rivers of anger and terrible pinnacle
bubbling from my furious, ill-fated being
toward the decline of a trembling, threatened fountain
that I strike with furious blows of
my fist at a thousand miles an hour.

"They called for you ...
Is he there?, they asked;
we laughed at your incredible adventure,
but the gentle voice broke into hoarse sobs
on the pink long distance telephone."

I DREAM that perhaps I will manage to exist,
but two o'clock in the early morning
is a hard patrol of implacable helmets
on dirty August cushions
striking the solitary temple shaped like
destiny's starving metropolises.

"He isn't here ...,
he isn't here ..., we said,
and the thick wire dissolved into opaque deafness,
and a galopping, wounded winter swooped down
on the pink long distance telephone."

SILENCE my depth of ruin
and the cry in my cavern corrodes into vitriol.
Thus my bronchial tubes
have become tiny putrified rats
and my hope, a suicidal sling,
an ardent collapse.

"Colgaron;
quedó un rumor de monstruos submarinos
platicando de caos con el helado pájaro del éter ...
Colgaron por las lejanías teléfonos color de rosa."

CONCLUYO y me emborracho
de valses cursis y cerveza de hormiga.
Me embriago en ventanales altos como mi desdicha
de permisionario de crepúsculo y booguie.
Un mendigo profundo me mira fijamente.
Perdido estoy. Mi martirio os ofrezco.
Mi voz descuartizada con tristeza fulmino.
Mi desvelar sangriento de arrojado.

"They hung up,
leaving the sound of submarine monsters
talking of chaos with the frozen bird of eter ...
They hung up on the pink long distance telephone."

I FINISH and I get drunk
on pretentious waltzes and ant beer.
I become intoxicated in windows as high as my
idle soldier's sunset and boogy mistery.
A profound beggar is staring at me.
I am lost. I offer you my martyrdom.
With my voice quartered by sorrow I fulminate.
My brave bloody insomnia.

E. L .T. Mesens

Edouard Léon Théodore Mesens (1903–71) was a Belgian collagist, poet, composer, art dealer, exhibition organizer, and collector. Born and raised in Brussels, he developed a special interest in contemporary painting, especially that associated with Dada and Surrealism. A friend of René Magritte, whose art he vigorously championed, he co-founded the Belgian Surrealist Group in 1926. Visiting Paris on numerous occasions between 1927 and 1937, Mesens kept the Brussels group constantly informed about the activities of the French Surrealists and vice versa. On the eve of World War II, Mesens settled in London, where he became the director of the London Gallery, and editor of the London Bulletin, which provided an important forum for Surrealism in England.

Fausse Vacance

Le printemps chauve arrête les bougies
Et les arbres à mirlitons

C'était un printemps pareil aux ourlets
Des persiennes closes au cadran du bonheur
Un printemps de chaise à porteurs
Un grand vide pour les poupées mécaniques

Et les marchands de pianos
Les bâtisseurs de murailles monotones
Ecumaient comme des chevaux de labor

Un régiment de brosses à dents
Attendait l'heure du bivouac

A cheval sur la chaîne de montagnes
Qui servait d'horizon au paysage
Un personnage gigantesque étendait les bras
Signe de lassitude

Le printemps chauve arrête les bougies
Et les arbres–bras dessus bras dessoous–
S'en vont en chuchotant.

False Vacation

The bald springtime halts the candles
And the trees with toy flutes

It was a hem-like springtime
Venetian blinds concealing the dial of happiness
A sedan chair springtime
A great void for the mechanical dolls

And the piano merchants
The builders of monotonous walls
Were foaming at the mouth like draft horses

A regiment of toothbrushes
Was waiting to bivouac

Astride the mountain chain
That served as the landscape's horizon
A gigantic individual stretched out his arms
A sign of fatigue

The bald springtime halts the candles
And the trees–arm in arm–
Whisper as they go away.

Proclamation

C'en est fait Messieurs!
Déjà les mannequins de cire envahissent les bibliothèques
Les femmes marchent comme des drapeaux mouillés
Les fous distribuent l'image de leur esprit
Aux portes des églises désaffectées

Rire
Je vous défends de rire ou de grincer des dents
Je vous défends de vendre vos chansons d'amour

Semez vox oripeaux
Mangez des fleurs et des fusées
Mêlez vos aliments à ceux des animaux
Et donnez-leur le tout et le reste de coeur

Ne conduisez plus vos enfants à l'école
Apprenez-leur l'usage SECRET
De la parole

Nous avons déjà renversé les tables de multiplication
Nous ne rentrerons plus à la maison du crime
Nous sommes infatigables jusque dans le sommeil
Tenez-le vous pour dit

Aujourd'hui c'est
Autour du monde
Au
TOUR
du
MONDE.

Proclamation

Its' all over, gentlemen!
The wax mannequins are already invading the libraries
The women are walking like soggy flags
The madmen are distributing pictures of their minds
At the doors of disaffected churches

Laugh
I forbid you to laugh or to grind your teeth
I forbid you to sell your love songs

Scatter your tawdry finery
Consume some flowers and some flares
Mingle your food with that of the animals
And give them all of it and the rest willingly

Stop driving your children to school
Teach them the SECRET practice
Of words

We have overturned the multiplication tables
We refuse to return to the place of the crime
We are tireless even in our sleep
Consider yourself warned

Today it is
Around the world
A
ROUND
the
WORLD

Le Mari Aride

Ma statue adorée

Le sol si dur à l'ordinaire
Et l'aile suspendue à un cri

Miraculeusement font place
A un sol mou
A une chanson fade et perpétuelle

Je t'ai tellement aimée
Que mon tailleur lui-même
Ne me reconnaît plus

Je t'ai tellement voulue
Que le lampiste ne passe plus
Par notre maison
Je t'ai construite sauvagement
Et sans arrière-pensée

Maintenant que le cadran
Marque toutes les heures une heure de moins
Que d'avantage en avantage
L'on perd à qui mieux mieux
Je suis pour toi pour tous
Le sac au dos
Le maréchal sans honte
Le colibri sans amertume

Le triangle ne trouvant pas où se placer
La brute inavouée
Le moralisateur sans gloire

The Arid Husband

My adorable statue

The ground which is ordinarily so hard
And the wing hanging on a cry

Yield miraculously
To soft ground
To a dull, perpetual song

I have loved you so intensely
That even my tailor
No longer recognizes me

I have so wanted
The lamp-lighter to stop coming
By our house
I have constructed you savagely
and without a backward thought

Now that the clockface
Subtracts an hour from the time
Now that competition is useless
more and more
I am for you for everyone
The backpack
The shameless blacksmith
The unembittered humming bird

The triangle uncertain as to where it belongs
The unavowed brute
The moraliser without glory

Et crois
Ma chère statue de gomme
A l'affection sans rives
De ton époux définitif
Ton vrai mari aride.

La Condition De L'homme Dépend De La Façon Dont Il Allume Sa Loupe

Vous qui luttez
Vous qui luttez la tartine à la main
Vous qui bataillez le toast au caviar brandi menaçant
Vous qui hurlez demi doublé demi fendu demi et turlutu
Arrêtez-vous

Il n'y a pas de lutte
Il n'y a pas de camps rivaux
Il n'y a que toi et toi et toi
        et moi
        dans le jardin de pois
        et toi et moi
        sur le chemin où s'impriment nos pas
        jusqu'à la prochaine pluie

Il n'y a que choux et dentelles
Il n'y a que vinaigrette de veau
Il n'y a que têtes de pavés
        pour les enfants des petits pavots
Il y a bon et mauvais pot

My dear rubber statue
Trust
In the boundless affection
Of your definitive spouse
Your true arid husband.

Man's Fate Depends on How He Lights his Magnifying Glass

You who are fighting
You who fight with bread and butter in hand
You who brandish your caviar toast menacingly
You who shout half doubled over half split in half and fiddlesticks
Stop

There is no fight
There are no rival camps
There is only you and you and you
 and I
 in the vegetable garden
 and you and I
 on the path where our footprints linger
 until the next rain

There are only cabbages and lacework
There is only veal vinaigrette
There are only cobblestone heads
 for the troublesome kids
There are good and bad pots

Il n'y a faucille ni marteau
Il y a enclume et fer chaud

Messieurs
Il n'y a pas de lard
Pour celui qui mange à merveille

Mesdames
Il n'y a pas d'art
Pour le merviellard.

Pour Mettre Fin à L'Age Des Machines Les Poètes Anglais Font De La Fumée

Voici des fleurs d'hiver
Voici des fleurs d'été
Du commerce et des poux
Des pralines et des bombes
Le tout donné vendu
Prêté acheté jeté

Les hommes ne tremblent plus
Puisqu'ils ont de grands maîtres
Qui pensent pour eux
Et prévoient tout

Les curés et les fous
Coiffés d'une salade
Jouent au nain jaune
Dans des lieux occultés

There are neither sickles nor hammers
There are anvils and hot irons

Gentlemen
There is no bacon
For one who eats like four

Ladies
There is little to be taken
From one who is four-saken.

In Order to Conclude the Machine age English Poets are Creating a Smokescreen

Here are some winter flowers
Here are some summer flowers
Some business and some lice
Some pralines and some bombs
Everything given sold
Loaned bought thrown away

Men no longer tremble
Because they have great masters
Who think for them
And foresee everything

Priests and madmen
Crowned with salads
Play cards
In obscure places

The red soldiers

Les soldats rouges
Sont commandés par des généraux beiges
Les soldats du sang
Sont commandés par moi

Stratégie de replis
Avale ta pilule.

Are commanded by beige generals
The blood's soldiers
Are commanded by me

Withdrawal strategy
Swallow your bitter pill.

César Moro

Born in Lima, Peru, César Moro (1903–56) was a pseudonym adopted by César Quispes Asín when he began to write poetry. Arriving in Paris in 1925, he discovered the Surrealists, enthusiastically adopted their cause, and participated in their activities. When he returned to Lima, eight years later, he strove to transplant Surrealism to his native soil. In 1935, Moro and Emilio Adolfo Wesphalen organized The First Latin American Surrealist Exhibition. Together with Manuel Moreno Jimeno, they also founded a Surrealist journal called *El Uso de la Palabra* (*The Use of the Word*) (1939). By the time it appeared, however, Moro had moved to Mexico, where he remained for the next ten years, engaged in numerous Surrealist activities. During his stay, he published two books of poems in French: *Le Château de Grisou* (1943) and *Lettre d'amour* (1944), and wrote a number of poems in Spanish. These were published posthumously, a year after his death, as *La tortuga ecuestre* (*The Equestrian Tortoise*) (1957).

El Olor Y La Mirada

El olor fino solitario de tu axilas

Un hacinamiento de coronas de paja y heno fresco cortado con dedos y asfodelos y piel fresca y galopes lejanos como perlas

Tu olor de cabellera bajo el agua azul con peces negros y estrellas de mar y estrellas de cielo bajo la nieve incalculable de tu mirada.

Tu mirada de holoturia de ballena de pedernal de lluvia de diarios de suicidas húmedos los ojos de tu mirada de pie de madrépora

Esponja diurna a medida que el mar escupe ballenas enfermas y cada escalera rechaza a su viandante como la bestia apestada que puebla los sueños del viajero

Y golpes centelleantes sobre las sienes y la ola que borra las centellas para dejar sobre el tapiz la eterna cuestión de tu mirada de objeto muerto tu mirada podrida de flor

El Mundo Ilustrado

Igual que tu ventana que no existe

Como una sombra de mano en un instrumento fantasma

Igual que las venas y el recorrido intenso de tu sangre

Con la misma igualdad con la continuidad preciosa que me asegura idealmente tu existencia

The Scent and the Gaze

The fine, solitary scent of your armpits

Stacked crowns of straw and freshly cut hay with fingers and asphodels and fresh skin and distant gallops like pearls

Your scent of hair beneath the blue water with black fish and starfish and celestial stars beneath the incalculable snow of your gaze

Your sea-slug gaze, like a whale, flint, rain, newspapers, damp suicides, your eyes with their white coral foot gaze

Daily sponge as the sea spits forth sick whales, and each staircase rejects its climber like the pestilential animal inhabiting the traveler's dreams

And flashing blows on the temples and the wave erasing the flashes, leaving on the carpet the eternal question of your dead object gaze, your rotten flower gaze

The Illustrated World

The same as your non-existent window

Like a hand's shadow in a phantom instrument

The same as your veins and your blood's intense journey

With the same equality with the precious continuity that ideally reassures me of your existence

A una distancia

A la distancia

A pesar de la distancia

Con tu frente y tu rostro

Y toda tu presencia sin cerrar los ojos

Y el paisaje que brota de tu presencia cuando la ciudad no era
no podía ser sino el reflejo inútil de tu presencia de
hecatombe

Para mejor mojar las plumas de la aves

Cae esta lluvia de muy alto

Y me encierra dentro de ti a mí solo

Dentro y lejos de ti

Como un camino que se pierde en otro continente

Westphalen

Como un abrevadero de bestias indelebles
Partido por el rayo desbordando el agua
Refleja la migración de las aves de tierra
En la noche de tierra salobre

Un portón cerrado sobre un campo baldío
Refugio del amor clandestino
Una igualdad de piedra que se cierra bajo
La gota de agua que sube de la tierra
Sobre centenares de cabezas decapitadas
Una mujer desnuda como una lámpara

At a distance

In the distance

Despite the distance

With your head and your face

And your entire presence without closing my eyes

And the landscape arising from your presence when the city was only, could only be, the useless reflection of your slaughter presence

In order to better moisten the birds' feathers

The rain is falling a great distance

And it encloses me within you all by myself

Within and far from you

Like a road that vanishes on another continent

Westphalen

Like a drinking trough for indelible animals
Divided by the overflowing beam of light the water
Reflects the migration of the world's birds
In the brackish earthen night

A large door shut on a wasteland
Refuge of clandestine love
An equality of stone closing beneath
The drop of water emerging from the earth
Above hundreds of decapitated heads
A woman naked as a lightbulb

Hace brillar los ojos de los muertos
Como peces decaudas de fibrillas argentiferas
El oro y el hierro conocen su destino
De tierra podrida el pulular de la selva
Le acompaña y vierte sobre los hombros
De los fantasmas familiares mantos arborescentes
Cascadas de sangre y miríadas de narices

André Breton

Como un piano de cola de caballo de cauda de estrellas
Sobre el firmamento lúgubre
Pesado de sangre coagulada
Arremolinando nubes arco-iris falanges de planetas y miríadas de aves
El fuego indeleble avanza
Los cipreses arden los tigres las panteras y los animales nobles se tornan incandescentes

El cuidado del alba ha sido abandonado
Y la noche se cierne sobre la tierra devastada

La comarca de tesoros guarda para siempre su nombre

Causes the eyes of the dead to shine
Like fish trailing silvery fibrils
Gold and iron know his destiny
Anchored in the rotten earth the swarming jungle
Accompanies him and spills arborescent cloaks
Waterfalls of blood and myriads of noses
On the familiar phantoms' shoulders

André Breton

Like a grand piano with a horse's tail, with stars' trails
In the gloomy firmament
Heavy with coagulated blood
Whirling clouds, rainbows, phalanxes of planets, and myriads of birds
The indelible fire advances
The cypresses burn the tigers, the panthers, and the noble animals turn incandescent

Dawn's caution has been abandoned
And night hovers above the devastated earth

The treasure vault guards his name forever

Libertad–Igualdad

El invierno recrudece la melancolía de la tortuga ecuestre
El invierno la viste de armio sangriento
El invierno tiene pies de madera y ojos de zapato
La esmeralda puede resistir la presencia insólita del tigre
Acoplado a la divina tortuga ecuestre
Con el bramido de la selva llorando por el ojo fatal de la amatista
La generación sublime por venir

Desata las uñas de las orquídeas que se clavan en la cabeza de los
angélicos ofidios

La divina tortuga asciende al cielo de la selva
Seguida por el tigre alado que duerme reclinada la cabeza sobre
una almohada viviente de tenuirrostros

El invierno famélico se vuelve un castillo
El invierno tiene orejas de escalera un peinado de cañón
Tiene dientes en forma de sillas de agua
Para que los soldados ecuestres de la tortuga
Beban las sillas y suban las orejas
Desbordantes de mensajes escritos en la nieve
Como aquel que dice: "a su muy digno cargo elevado
Como el viento participe en un % mínimo, me es grato
Dirigir un alerta de silencio"

En vano los ojos se cansan de mirar
La divina pareja embarcada en la cópula
Boga interminable entre las ramas de la noche
De tiempo en tiempo un volcán estalla
Con cada gemido de la diosa
Bajo el tigre real

Liberty–Equality

Winter worsens the equestrian tortoise's melancholy
Winter dresses him in bloodstained ermine
Winter has wooden feet and shoe eyes
The emerald can resist the tiger's unexpected presence
Coordinated with the divine equestrian tortoise
With the jungle loudly lamenting the amethyst's fatal eye

The sublime future generation loosens the orchids' claws
embedded in the angelic serpents' heads

The divine tortoise ascends to the jungle's sky
Followed by the winged tiger sleeping with its head on a living
pillow of birds

The famished winter turns into a castle
Winter has staircase ears, a canyon hairstyle
It has teeth in the shape of water chairs
So the tortoise's equestrian soldiers
Can drink the chairs and raise their ears
Overflowing with messages written in the snow
For example: "in its very worthy charge the wind participates in a
minimum %, I am pleased
To direct a silent alert"

In vain eyes grow tired of looking
The divine couple engaged in copulation
Sail interminably among the night's branches
From time to time a volcano erupts
With each of the goddess' moans
Beneath the royal tiger

Pablo Neruda

Born in Parral, Chile, Pablo Neruda (1904–73) was a pseudonym adopted by Neftalí Ricardo Reyes Basoalto when he began to write poetry. Entitled *La canción de la fiesta* (*The Song of the Festival*), his first book of poems appeared in 1921, followed by a many more volumes over the years. In 1927, Neruda began his long career as a Chilean diplomat. Stationed in Buenos Aires, in 1933, he became friends with Federico García Lorca, who was directing a production of *Bodas de sangre* (*Blood Wedding*) there. During his lifetime, Neruda wrote many different kinds of poetry, including historical epics, political manifestos, poems in prose, lyrical exercises, passionate love poems, and Surrealist poems. In *Residencia en la tierra* (*Residence on Earth*), written between 1925 and 1935, he adopted Surrealist techniques in order to explore his turbulent unconscious. With the outbreak of the Spanish Civil War the following year, Neruda began to write the powerful political poetry for which he is especially known. In 1971, he received the Nobel Prize in Literature.

Arte Poética

Entre sombra y espacio, entre guarniciones y doncellas,
dotado de corazón singular y sueños funestos,
precipitadamente pálido, marchito en la frente
y con luto de viudo furioso por cada día de mi vida,
ay, para cada agua invisible que bebo soñolientamente
y de todo sonido que acojo temblando,
tengo la misma sed ausente y la misma fiebre fría
un oído que nace, una angustia indirecta,
como si llegaran ladrones o fantasmas,
y en una cáscara de extensión fija y profunda,
como un camarero humillado, como una campana un poco
ronca,
como un espejo viejo, como un olor de casa sola
en la que los huéspedes entran de noche perdidamente
ebrios,
y hay un olor de ropa tirada al suelo, y una ausencia de
flores
—posbilemente de otro modo aún menos melancólico—,
pero, la verdad, de pronto, el viento que azota mi pecho,
las noches de substancia infinita caídas en mi dormitorio,
el ruido de un día que arde con sacrificio
me piden lo profético que hay en mí, con melancolía
y un golpe de objetos que llaman sin ser respondidos
hay, y un movimiento sin tregua, y un nombre confuso.

The Art of Poetry

Between shadow and space, between ornaments and
damsels,
endowed with a singular heart and disastrous dreams,
precipitately pallid, withered in the forehead
and with a widower's furious mourning for each day of life,
oh, for each invisible water that I drink somnolently,
and for every sound that I welcome trembling,
I have the same absent thirst and the same cold fever,
a nascent ear, and indirect anguish,
as if robbers or phantoms had arrived,
and in a shell of constant and profound dimensions,
like a humiliated waiter, like a slightly hoarse bell,
like an old mirror, like an odor from a lone house
that harbors dead drunk guests at night,
and there is an odor of clothes thrown on the floor, and no
flowers,
—possibly in another even less melancholy manner—,
but the truth, suddenly, the wind whipping my chest,
the nights of infinite substance fallen in my bedroom,
the noise of a day burning with sacrifice
ask sadly for the prophetic within me,
and there are a bunch of objects that call without being
answered,
and a continual movement, and a confused man.

Cantares

La parracial rosa devora
y sube a la cima del santo:
con espesas garras sujeta
el tiempo al fatigado ser:
hincha y sopla en las venas duras,
ata el cordel pulmonar, entonces
largamente escucha y respira.

Morir deseo, vivir quiero,
herramienta, perro infinito,
movimiento de océano espeso
con vieja y negra superficie.

Para quién y a quién en la sombra
mi gradual guitarra resuena
naciendo en la sal de mi ser
como el pez en la sal del mar?

Ay, qué continuo país cerrado,
neutral, en la zona del fuego,
inmóvil, en el giro terrible,
seco, en la humedad de las cosas.

Entonces, entre mis rodillas,
bajo la raíz de mis ojos,
prosigue cosiendo mi alma:
su aterradora aguja trabaja.

Sobrevivo en medio del mar,
solo y tan locamente herido,
tan solamente persistiendo,
heridamente abandonado.

Songs

The parracial rose devours
and climbs to the top of the saint:
with thick claws it attaches
time to the weary being:
it swells up and inflates the hard veins,
it ties off the pulmonary cord, then
listens and breathes at great length.

I want to die, I want to live,
tool, infinite dog,
thick ocean movement
with an old black surface.

For whom and to whom in the shade
does my gradual guitar sound,
arising from the salt of my being
like a fish in the salt of the sea?

Oh, what a continuous closed country,
neutral, in the zone of fire,
immobile, in the terrible spinning,
dry, in the humidity of things.

Then, between my knees,
beneath my eyes' roots,
my soul continues to sew:
its fearful needle works away.

I survive in the middle of the sea,
alone and so insanely wounded,
so solely persisting,
woundedly abandoned.

Agua Sexual

Rodando a goterones solos,
a gotas como dientes,
a espesos goterones de mermelada y sangre,
rodando a goterones,
cae el agua,
como una espada en gotas,
como un desgarrador río de vidrio,
cae mordiendo,
golpeando el eje de la simetría, pegando en las costuras del alma,
rompiendo cosas abandonadas, empapando lo oscuro.

Solamente es un soplo, más húmedo que el llanto,
un líquido, un sudor, un aceite sin nombre,
un movimiento agudo,
haciéndose, espesándose,
cae el agua,
a goterones lentos,
hacia su mar, hacia su seco océano,
hacia su ola sin agua.

Veo el verano extenso, y un estertor saliendo de un granero,
bodegas, cigarras,
poblaciones, estímulos,
habitaciones, niñas
durmiendo con las manos en el corazón,
soñando con bandidos, con incendios,
veo barcos,
eo árboles de médula
erizados como gatos rabiosos,

Sexual Water

Rolling in big solitary drops,
in drops like teeth,
in big thick drops of marmelade and blood,
rolling in big drops,
the water falls,

In drops like a sword,
like a tearing river of glass,
it falls biting,
striking the symmetrical axis, clinging to the soul's seams,
breaking abandoned objects, soaking the darkness.

It is only a breath, moister than tears,
a liquid, a sweat, an anonymous oil,
a sharp movement,
taking form, gathering thickness,
the water falls,
in big slow drops,
toward its sea, toward its dry ocean,
toward its waterless wave.

I see the vast summer, and a death rattle emerging from a granary,
warehouses, cicadas,
towns, stimuli,
rooms, girls
sleeping with their hand- on their heart-,
dreaming of bandits, of fires,
I see ships,

veo sangre, puñales y medias de mujer,
y pelos de hombre,
veo camas, veo corredores donde grita una virgen,
veo frazadas y órganos y hoteles.

Veo les sueños sigilosos,
admito los postreros días,
y también los orígenes, y también los recuerdos,
como un párpado atrozmente levantado a la fuerza
estoy mirando.

Y entonces hay este sonido:
un ruido rojo de huesos,
un pegarse de carne,
y piernas amarillas como espigas juntándose.
Yo escucho entre el disparo de los besos,
escucho, sacudido entre respiraciones y sollozos.

Estoy, mirando, oyendo,
con la mitad del alma en el mar y la mitad del alma en la tierra,
y con las dos mitades del alma miro el mundo.

Y aunque cierre los ojos y me cubra el corazón enteramente,
veo caer agua sorda,
a goterones sordos.
Es como un huracán de gelatina,
como una catarata de espermas y medusas.
Veo correr un arco iris túrbio.
Veo pasar sus aguas a través de los huesos.

I see pulp trees
bristling like rabid cats,
I see blood, daggers, and women's stockings,
and men's hair,
I see beds, I see corridors where a virgin screams,
I see blankets and organs and hotels.

I see secret dreams,
I recognize final days,
and also origins, and also memories,
like an eyelid atrociously and forcibly exposed
I am looking.

And then there is this sound:
a red noise of bones,
a joining of flesh
and yellow legs like ears of grain side by side.
And I listen among the explosion of kisses,
I listen, shaken between gasps and sobs.
I am looking, hearing,
with half my soul at sea and half my soul on land,
and with the two halves of my soul I examine the world.

And although I close my eyes and cover my heart entirely,
I see a muffled water fall,
in big muffled drops.
It is like a hurricane of gelatine,
like a waterfall of sperm and jellyfish.
I see a misty rainbow suddenly appear.
I see its waters pass across the bones.

Apogeo Del Apio

Del centro puro que los ruidos nunca
atravesaron, de la intacta cera,
salen claros relámpagos lineales,
palomas con destino de volutas,
hacia tardías calles con olor
a sombra y a pescado.

Son las venas del apio! Son la espuma, la risa,
los sombreros del apio!
Son los signos del apio, su sabor
de luciérnaga, sus mapas
de color inundado,
y cae su cabeza de ángel verde,
y sus delgados rizos se acongojan,
y entran los pies del apio en los mercados
de la mañana herida, entre sollozos,
y se cierran las puertas a su paso,
y los dulces caballos se arrodillan.

Sus pies cortados van, sus ojos verdes,
van derramados, para siempre hundidos
en ellos los secretos y las gotas:
los túneles del mar de donde emergen,
las escaleras que el apio aconseja,
las desdichadas sombras sumergidas,
las determinaciones en el centro del aire,
los besos en el fondo de las piedras.

A medianoche, con manos mojadas,
alguien golpea mi puerta en la niebla,

The Apogee of Celery

From the pure center the noises never
penetrated, from the intact wax,
come clear linear flashes of lightning,
doves with a spiral destiny,
toward tardy streets smelling
of shadows and fish.

These are the celery's veins! They are the foam, the laughter,
the celery's hats!
They are the celery's signs, its glow-worm
taste, its maps
of flooded color,
and its green angel head tumbles,
and its thin curls grow sad,
and the celery's feet enter the markets
of the wounded morning, between sobs,
and the doors close as they pass,
and the gentle horses kneel.

The amputated feet, the green eyes
are spread out, secrets and drops
forever sunk in them:
the sea's tunnels from which they emerge,
the staircases that the celery advises,
the poor submerged shadows,
the resolutions in the center of the air,
the kisses at the bottom of the stones.

At midnight, with wet hands,
someone knocks at my door in the fog,

y oigo la voz del apio, voz profunda,
áspera voz de viento encarcelado,
se queja herido de aguas y raíces,
hunde en mi cama sus amargos rayos,
y sus desordenadas tijeras me pegan en el pecho
buscándome la boca del corazón ahogado.

¿Qué quieres, huésped de corsé quebradizo,
en mis habitaciones funerales?
¿Qué ámbito destrozado te rodea?

Fibras de oscuridad y luz llorando,
ribetes ciegos, energías crespas,
río de vida y hebras essenciales,
verdes ramas de sol acariciado,
aquí estoy, en la noche, escuchando secretos,
desvelos, soledades,
y entráis, en medio de la niebla hundida,
hasta crecer en mí, hasta comunicarme
la luz oscura y la rosa de la tierra.

Oda a Federico García Lorca

Si pudiera llorar de miedo en una casa sola,
si pudiera sacarme los ojos y comérmelos,
lo haría por tu voz de naranjo enlutado
y por tu poesia que sale dando gritos.

Porque por ti pintan de azul los hospitales
y crecen las escuelas y los barrios marítimos,
y se pueblan de plumas los ángeles heridos,

and I hear the celery's voice, a deep voice,
a harsh voice of imprisoned wind,
it moans wounded by waters and roots,
its bitter rays sink into my bed,
and its unruly scissors stick me in the chest,
seeking the mouth of my drowned heart.

What do you want, guest with fragile corset,
in my dismal rooms?
What shattered sphere encloses you?

Fibers of darkness and weeping light,
blind trimmings, curly energies,
river of life and essential fibers,
green branches of cherished sun,
here I am, at night, listening to secrets,
insomnias, solitudes,
and you enter, surrounded by the sunken fog,
until you grow in me, until you reveal to me
the dark light and the earth's rose.

Ode to Federico García Lorca

If I could cry from fear in a solitary house,
if I could remove my eyes and eat them,
I would do it for your orange tree voice dressed in
mourning
and for your poety screaming as it emerges.

Because for you they paint hospitals blue,
and schools and dock areas grow larger,

y se cubren de escamas los pescados nupciales,
y van volando al cielo los erizos:
por ti sastrerías con sus negras membranas
se llenan de cucharas y de sangre
y tragan cintas rotas, y se matan a besos,
y se visten de blanco.

Cuando vuelas vestido de durazno,
cuando ríes con risa de arroz huracanado,
cuando para cantar sacudes las arterias y los dientes,
la garganta y los dedos,
me moriría por los lagos rojos
en donde en medio del otoño vives
con un corcel caído y un dios ensangrentado,
me moriría por los cementerios
que como cenicientos ríos pasan
con agua y tumbas,
de noche, entre campanas ahogadas:
ríos espesos como dormitorios
de soldados enfermos, que de súbito crecen
hacia la muerte en ríos con números de mármol
y coronas podridas, y aceites funerales:
me moriría por verte de noche
mirar pasar las cruces anegadas,
de pie llorando,
porque ante el río de la muerte lloras
abandonadamente, heridamente,
lloras llorando, con los ojos llenos
de lágrimas, de lágrimas, de lágrimas.

Si pudiera de noche, perdidamente solo,
acumular olvido y sombra y humo

and wounded angels deck themselves with feathers,
and nuptial fish cover themselves with scales,
and hedgehogs go flying away:
for you tailor-shops with their black membranes
fill up with spoons and with blood,
and swallow red ribbons, and kiss each other to death,
and put on white clothes.

When you fly around dressed as a peach,
when you laugh with a laughter of hurricaned rice,
when preparing to sing you shake your arteries and your
teeth,
your throat and your fingers,
I feel like dying you are so sweet,
I feel like dying for the red lakes
where you live in mid autumn
with a fallen steed and a bloodied god,
I feel like dying for the cemeteries
that pass by like ashen rivers
with water and tombs,
at night, among drowned bells:
rivers as thick as barracks with
sick soldiers, which suddenly grow
toward death in rivers with marble numbers
and rotting crowns, and funeral oils:
I feel like dying to see you at night
watching the flooded crosses go by,
standing and crying,
because before the river of death you cry
sadly, woundedly,
you cry crying, with your eyes full
of tears, tears, tears.

sobre ferrocarriles y vapores,
con un embudo negro,
mordiendo las cenizas,
lo haría por el árbol en que creces,
por los nidos de aguas doradas que reúnes,
y por la enredadera que te cubre los huesos
comunicándote el secreto de la noche.

Ciudades con olor a cebolla mojada
esperan que tú pases cantando roncamente,
y silenciosos barcos de esperma te persiguen,
y golondrinas verdes hacen nido en tu pelo,
y además caracoles y semanas,
mátiles enrollados y cerezas
definitivamente circulan cuando asoman
tu pálida cabeza de quince ojos
y tu boca de sangre sumergida.

Si pudiera llenar de hollín las alcaldías
y, sollozando, derribar relojes,
sería para ver cuando a tu casa
llega el verano con los labios rotos,
llegan muchas personas de traje agonizante,
llegan regiones de triste esplendor,
llegan arados muertos y amapolas,
llegan enterradores y jinetes,
llegan planetas y mapas con sangre
llegan buzos cubiertos de ceniza,
llegan enmascarados arrastrando doncellas
atravesadas por grandes cuchillos,
llegan raíces, venas, hospitales,
manantiales, hormigas,

If at night, hopelessly alone, I could
amass oblivion and shadow and smoke
above railroads and steamships,
with a black funnel,
biting the ashes,
I would do it for the tree in which you grow,
for the nests of the golden waters that you join together,
and for the convolvulus covering your bones
imparting the night's secret to you.

Cities that smell like wet onions
wait for you to pass singing hoarsely,
and silent boats of sperm pursue you,
and green swallows make their nests in your hair,
and also snails and weeks,
wrapped masts and cherry trees
finally make the rounds when
your pale head with fifteen eyes
and your mouth of submerged blood appear.

If I could fill townhalls with soot
and, sobbing, demolish clocks,
it would be to see your house
when summer arrives,with broken lips
when crowds of people with moribund clothing arrive,
when regions of sad splendor arrive,
when dead plays and poppies arrive.
when gravediggers and horsemen arrive,
when planets and bloody maps arrive,
when buzzards covered with ashes arrive,
when masked men arrive dragging damsels
pierced by large knives,

llega la noche con la cama en donde
muere entre las arañas un húsar solitario,
llega una rosa de odio y alfileres,
llega una embarción amarillenta,
llega un día de viento con un niño,
llego yo con Oliverio, Norah,
Vicente Aleixandre, Delia,
Maruca, Malva Marina, María Luisa y Larco,
la Rubia, Rafael Ugarte,
Cotapos, Rafael Alberti,
Carlos, Bebé, Manolo Altolaguirre,
Molinari,
Rosales, Concha Méndez,
y otros que se me olvidan.
Ven a que te corone, joven de la salud
y de la mariposa, joven puro
como un negro relámpago perpetuamente libre,
y conversando entre nosotros,
ahora, cuando no queda nadie entre las rocas,
hablemos sencillamente como eres tú y soy yo:
para qué sirven los versos si no es para el rocio?

Para qué sirven los versos si no es para esa noche
en que un puñal amargo nos averigua, para ese día,
para ese crepúsculo, para ese rincón roto
donde el golpeado corazón del hombre se dispone a morir?

Sobre todo de noche,
de noche hay muchas estrellas,
todas dentro de un río
como una cinta junto a las ventanas
de las casas llenas de pobres gentes.

when roots, veins, hospital,
springs, ants arrive,
when night arrives with a bed where
a solitary hussar is dying among the spiders,
when a rose of hatred and pins arrives
when a yellowish boat arrives,
when a windy day with a boy arrives,
when I arrive with Oliverio, Norah,
Vicente Aleixandre, Delia,
Maruca, Malva Marina, María Luisa y Larco,
the Blond, Rafael Ugarte,
Cotapos, Rafael Alberti,
Carlos, Bebé, Manolo Altolaguerre,
Molinari,
Rosales, Concha Méndez,
and others whom I forget.

Come, let me crown you, youth of health
and butterflies, youth pure
as a flash of black lightning perpetually free,
and speaking among ourselves,
now, when no one remains among the rocks,
let us speak simply, just us two:
what are verses good for if not the dew?

What are verses good for if not the night when
a bitter dagger probes us, for the day,
for the dusk, for the broken corner
where a man's beaten heart prepares to die?

Above all at night,
at night there are many stars,
all within a river

Alguien se les ha muerto, tal vez
han perdido sus colocaciones en las oficinas,
en los hospitales, en los ascensores,
en las minas,
sufren los seres tercamente heridos
y hay propósito y llanto en todas partes:
mientras las estrellas corren dentro de un río interminable
hay mucho llanto en las ventanas,
los umbrales están gastados por el llanto,
las alcobas están mojadas por el llanto
que llega en forma de ola a morder las alfombras.

Federico,
tú ves el mundo, las calles,
el vinagre,
las despedidas en las estaciones
cuando el humo levanta sus ruedas decisivas
hacia donde no hay nada sino algunas
separaciones, piedras, vías férreas.

Hay tantas gentes haciendo preguntas
por todas partes,
Hay el ciego snagriento, y el iracundo, y el
desanimado,
y el miserable, el árbol de las uñas,
el bandolero con la envidia a cuestas.

Así es la vida, Federico, aquí tienes
las cosas que te puede ofrecer mi amistad
de melancólico varón varonil.
Ya sabes por ti mismo muchas cosas,
y otras irás sabiendo lentamente.

like a ribbon near the windows
of houses full of poor people.

One of them has died, perhaps
they have lost their jobs in the offices,
in the hospitals, in the elevators,
in the mines,
human beings suffer stubbornly wounded
and there are projects and tears everywhere:
while the stars flow within an endless river
there are many tears shed at windows,
thresholds are worn away by tears,
bedrooms are drenched with tears
that arrive in waves to bite the carpets.

Federico,
you see the world, the streets,
the vinegar,
the goodbyes in the stations
when smoke raises its decisive wheels
toward nothing but
gaps, stones, railroad tracks

There are so many people asking questions
everywhere.
There is the bloody blindman, and the irascible man,
    and the dejected man,
and the wretched man, the thorn tree,
the bandit with envy on his back.

That's the way life goes, Federico, here you have
the things my friendship can offer you,
the friendship of a melancholy manly man.
You already know many things yourself,
and you will gradually come to know others.

Octavio Paz

Born and raised in Mexico City, Octavio Paz (1914–98) was a career diplomat who authored twenty-four books of poetry during his lifetime, besides a great many volumes of prose. Encouraged by Pablo Neruda, he published an avant-garde journal called *Barandal (Balustrade)* in 1931, and his first book of poetry, *Luna silvestre* (*Savage Moon*), in 1933. Paz first became aware of Surrealism in 1936, when he came across an article by André Breton that, in his own words, "me abrió las puertas de la poesía moderna" ("opened the doors of modern poetry for me"). Ten years later, he was able to thank the author in person while serving as cultural attaché to the Mexican embassy in Paris. Assigned to the French capital from 1946 to 1950, Paz participated in numerous Surrealist activities during his stay, and developed a close relationship with Breton, who was highly impressed by his poetry. In 1990, the Swedish Academy concurred with his judgment, awarding Paz the Nobel Prize in Literature.

Fábula

A Álvaro Mutis

Edades de fuego y de aire
Mocedades de agua
Del verde al amarillo
                    Del amarillo al rojo
Del sueño a la vigilia
                    Del deseo al acto
Sólo había un paso que tú dabas sin esfuerzo
Los insectos eran joyas animadas
El calor reposaba al borde del estanque
La lluvia era un sauce de pelo suelto
En la palma de tu mano crecía un árbol
Aquel árbol cantaba reía y profetizaba
Sus vaticinios cubrían de alas el espacio
Había milagros sencillos llamados pájaros
                    Todo era de todos
Todos eran todo
Sólo había una palabra inmensa y sin revés
Palabra como un sol
Un día se rompió en fragmentos diminutos
Son las palabras del lenguaje que hablamos
Fragmentos que nunca se unirán
Espejos rotos donde el mundo se mira destrozado

Fable

For Álvaro Mutis

Era of fire and era of air
Youthful waters
From green to yellow
From yellow to red
From dream to vigilance
From desire to action
was but a single step you took effortlessly
The insects were lively jewels
The heat rested on the edge of the pond
The rain was a willow with streaming hair
In the palm of your hand a tree was growing
That sang, laughed, and uttered prophesies
Its predictions covered the space with their wings
Simple miracles existed called birds
Everything was everybody's
Everybody was everything
Only one immense word existed with no antonym
A word like a sun
A day shattered into tiny pieces
That are the words of the language we speak
Pieces that will never be reunited
Shattered mirrors in which the world sees its smashed reflection

El Día Abre La Mano …

El día abre la mano
tres nubes
y estas pocas palabras

Refranes

Una espiga es todo el trigo
Una pluma es un pájaro vivo y cantando
Un hombre de carne es un hombre de sueño
La verdad no se parte
El trueno proclama los hechos del relámpago
Una mujer soñada encarna siempre en una forma amada
El árbol dormido pronuncia verdes oráculos
El agua habla sin cesar y nunca se repite
En la balanza de unos párpados el sueño no pesa
En la balanza de una lengua que delira
Una lengua de mujer que dice sí a la vida
El ave del paraíso abre las alas

Hacia El Poema (Puntos de Partida)

I

Palabras, ganancias de un cuarto de hora arrancado al árbol calcinado del lenguaje, entre los buenos días y las buenas noches, puertas de entrada y salida y entrada de un corredor que va de ningunparte a ningúnlado.

Day Opens its Hand ...

Day opens its hand
Three clouds
And these few words

Sayings

A single ear of wheat is worth the entire field
A single feather is worth a lively singing bird
A man of flesh is a man of dream
Truth rejects division
One clap of thunder proclaims the lightning's deeds
A dreaming woman assumes a beloved form
The sleeping tree pronounces green oracles
Water talks continually without repeating itself
Placed in the eyelids' balance dream weighs nothing
Placed on the scales of a raving tongue
A woman's tongue embraces life
The bird of paradise spreads its wings

Toward the Poem (Points of Departure)

I

Words, profits, of a quarter hour pried from the charred tree of language, between good mornings and good nights, entries and

Damos vueltas y vueltas en el vientre animal, en el vientre mineral, en el vientre temporal. Encontrar la salida: el poema.

Obstinación de ese rostro donde se quiebran mis miradas. Frente armada, invicta ante un paisaje en ruinas, tras el asalto al secreto. Melancolía de volcán. La benévola jeta de piedra de cartón del Jefe, del Conductor, fetiche del siglo; los yo, tú, él, tejedores de telarañas, pronombres armados de uñas; las divinidades sin rostro, abstractas. Él y nosotros, Nosotros y Él: nadie y ninguno. Dios padre se venga en todos estos ídolos.

El instante se congela, blancura compacta que ciega y no responde y se desvanece, témpano empujado por corrientes circulares. Ha de volver.

Arrancar las máscaras de la fantasía, clavar una pica en el centro sensible: provocar la erupción.

Cortar el cordón umbilical, matar bien a la Madre: crimen que el poeta moderno cometió por todos, en nombre de todos. Toca al nuevo poeta descubrir a la Mujer.

Hablar por hablar, arrancar sones a la desesperada, escribir al dictado lo que dice el vuelo de la mosca, ennegrecer. El tiempo se abre en dos: hora del salto mortal.

II

Palabras, frases sílabas, astros que giran alrededor de un centro fijo. Dos cuerpos, muchos seres que se encuentran en una palabra. El papel se cubre de letras indelebres, que nadie dijo, que nadie dictó, que han caído allí y arden y queman y se apagan. Así pues, existe la poesía, el amor existe. Y si yo no existo, existes tú.

exits and the entrance to a corridor leading from no place to nowhere.

We turn round and round in the animal belly, in the mineral belly, in the temporal belly. Discovering an exit: the poem.

That stubborn face where my glances lie shattered. Armed forehead, inviolate before a ruined landscape, following an attack on the secret. Volcanic melancholy.

The Chief's, the Leader's benevolent mug made of stone of cardboard, the century's fetish; I, you, he, spinners of spider webs, pronouns armed with claws; faceless, abstract divinities. He and me, We and He: no one and nobody. God the father wreaks vengeance on all these idols.

The instant freezes, a blinding compact whiteness that does not reply but disappears, an ice floe at the whim of circular currents. It will return.

Rip off fantasy's masks, plant a pike in feeling's center: provoke an eruption.

Sever the umbilical cord, put the Mother to death: a crime committed by the modern poet on behalf of everyone. The task of the new poet is to discover Woman.

Speaking for the sake of speaking, tear my sounds from the despairing woman, write down what the fly's flight dictates, blacken. Time splits in half: the hour of the somersault.

II

Words, phrases, syllables, stars wheeling around a fixed center. Two bodies, many beings who meet in a single word. The paper is covered with indelible letters, spoken by no one, dictated by no

Por todas partes los solitarios forzados empiezan a crear las palabras del nuevo diálogo.

El chorro de agua. La bocanada de salud. Una muchacha reclinada sobre su pasado. El vino, el fuego, la guitarra, la sobremesa. Un muro de terciopelo rojo en una plaza de pueblo. Las acalaciones, la caballería reluciente entrando a la ciudad, el pueblo en vilo: himnos! La irrupción de lo blanco, de lo verde, de lo llameante. Lo demasiado fácil, lo que se escribe solo: la poesía.

El poema prepara un orden amoroso. Preveo un hombre-sol y una mujer-luna, el uno libre de su poder, la otra libre de sus exclavitud, y amores implacables rayando el espacio negro. Todo ha de ceder a esas águilas incandescentes.

Por las almenas de tu frente el canto alborea. La justicia poética incendia campos de oprobio: no hay sitio para la nostalgia, el yo, el nombre proprio.

Todo poema se cumple a expensas del poeta.

Mediodía futuro, árbol inmenso de follaje invisible. En las plazas cantan los hombres y las mujeres el canto solar, surtidor de transparencias. Me cubre la marejada amarilla: nada mío ha de hablar por me boca.

Cuando la Historia duerme, habla en sueños: en la frente del pueblo dormido el poema es una constelación de sangre. Cuando la Historia despierta, la imagen se hace acto, acontece el poema: la poesía entra en acción.

Merece lo que sueñas.

one, fallen from nowhere, flaming, burning, and extinguished. In this way, therefore, poetry exists, love exists. And if I don't exist, you exist.

Gushing water. A mouthful of health. A girl leaning on her past. Wine, fire, a guitar, a tablecloth. A red velvet wall in a village square. Cheers, the glittering cavalry entering the town, the village bursting with suspense: hymns! Whiteness blazes forth coupled with green. That which is all too easy, that which writes itself: poetry.

The poem prepares a loving order. I foresee a sun-man and a moon-woman, he freed from his power, she freed from her slavery, and implacable loves illuminating black space. Everything yields before those incandescent eagles.

The song dawns over your forehead's battlements. Poetic justice sets fire to the fields of disgrace: no place remains for nostalgia, for the ego, for proper nouns.
Every poem is created at the poet's expense.

Future noon, immense tree with invisible foliage. In the squares men and women are singing the sun's song, a fountain of transparencies. The yellow waves cover me: nothing of mine needs to speak through my mouth.

When History sleeps, it speaks in dreams: on sleeping people's foreheads the poem is a constellation of blood. When History awakes, image becomes deed, the poem is born: poetry goes into action.

Strive to deserve your dreams.

El Prisionero
(Homenaje a D. A. F. de Sade)

à fin que … les traces de ma tombe disparaissent de dessus la surface de la terre comme je me flatte que ma mémoire s'éffacera de l'esprit des hommes …
Testamento de Sade

No te has desvanecido.
Las letras de tu nombre son todavía una cicatriz que no se cierra,
un tatuaje de infamia sobre ciertas frentes.
Cometa de pesada y rutilante cola dialéctica,
atraviesas el siglo diecinueve con una granada de verdad en la
mano
y estallas al llegar a nuestra época.

Máscara que sonríe bajo un antifaz rosa,
hecho de párpados de ajusticiado,
verdad partida en mil pedazos de fuego,
¿qué quieren decir todos esos fragmentos gigantescos,
esa manada de icebergs que zarpan de tu pluma y en alta mar
enfilan hacia costas sin nombre,
esos delicados instrumentos de cirugía para extirpar el chancro
de Dios,
esos aullidos que interrumpen tus majestuosos razonamientos de
elefante,
esas repeticiones atroces de relojería descompuesta,
toda esa oxidada herramienta de tortura?

El erudito y el poeta,
el sabio, el literato, el enamorado,

The Prisoner (Homage to D. A. F. Sade)

"so that … all traces of my grave vanish from
the face of the earth as I flatter myself that
my memory
will be obliterated in men's minds …"
—Sade's last will and testament

You have not vanished.
The letters of your name still form a scar that refuses to heal,
a tattoo of infamy on certain foreheads.

Weighty comet with your bright dialectical tail,
You zoom through the nineteenth century holding a grenade
finally exploding when you reach our era.

Mask that smiles beneath a pink surface,
composed of executed prisoners' eyelids,
truth divided into a thousand flames,
what do all those giant fragments mean?
that pack of icebergs emerging from your pen and heading
for nameless coasts across the high seas?
those delicate surgical instruments for excising the cancer of
God?
those howls interrupting your majestic elephantine thoughts?
those atrocious sounds of broken clockwork?
all those rusty tools of torture?

The intellectual and the poet,
the scholar, the man of letters, the lover,

el maníaco y el que sueña en la abolición de nuestra siniestra
realidad,
disputan como perros sobre los restos de tu obra.
Tú, que estabas contra todos,
eres ahora un nombre, un jefe, una bandera.

Inclinado sobre la vida como Saturno sobre sus hijos,
recorres con fija mirada amorosa
los surcos calcinados que dejan el semen, la sangre y la lava.
Los cuerpos, frente a frente como astros feroces,
están hechos de la misma substancia de los soles.
Lo que llamamos amor o muerte, libertad o destino,
¿no se llama catástrofe, no se llama hecatombe?
¿Dónde están las fronteras entre espasmo y terremoto,
entre erupción y cohabitación?

Prisionero en tu castillo de cristal de roca
cruzas galerías, cámaras, mazmorras,
vastos patios donde la vid se enrosca a columnas solares,
graciosos cementerios donde danzan los chopos inmóviles.
Muros, objetos, cuerpos te repiten.
Todo es espejo!
tu imagen te persigue.

El hombre está habitado por silencio y vacío.
¿Cómo saciar esta hambre,
cómo acallar y poblar su vacío
¿Cómo escapar a mi imagen?
Sólo en mi semejante me trasciendo,
sólo su sangre da fe de otra existencia.
Justina sólo vive pour Julieta,
las víctimas engendran los verdugos.

the maniac and the man dreaming of our sinister reality's
destruction,
fight like dogs over your work's last few scraps.
You who despised them all,
are today a name, a leader, and a banner.

Bent over life like Saturn over his sons,
you scan the roasted earth for traces of semen, blood, and lava
with your steady loving gaze.
Face to face like ferocious stars, our bodies
are made of the same substance as these suns.
What we call love or death, freedom or fate,
isn't it really catastrophe, isn't it slaughter?

Where are the boundaries between spasm and earthquake,
between eruption and orgasm?

Prisoner in your castle of rock crystal
you walk through galleries, rooms, and dungeons,
vast courtyards where vines coil about sunny columns,
gracious cemeteries where motionless poplars dance.
Wells, objects, bodies reflect you.
Everything is a mirror!
Your image pursues you everywhere.

Man is inhabited by silence and emptiness.
How can one satisfy this hunger,
how can one appease this silence and people its void?
How can I escape my image?
Only by transcending myself in my likeness,
only its blood attests to this other existence.
Justine lives only through Juliette,
victims engender their executioners.

El cuerpo que hoy sacrificamos
¿no es el Dios que mañana sacrifica?
La imaginación es la espuela del deseo,
su reino es inagotable e infinito como el fastidio,
su reverso y gemelo.

Muerte o placer, inundación o vómito,
otoño parecido al caer de los días,
volcán o sexo,
soplo, verano que incendia las cosechas,
astros o colmillos,
petrificada cabellera del espanto,
espuma roja des deseo, matanza en alta mar,
rocas azules del delirio,
formas, imágenes, burbujas, hambre de ser,
eternidades momentáneas,
desmesuras: tu medida de hombre.
Atrévete:
la libertad es la elección de la necesidad.
Sé el arco y la flecha, la cuerda y el ay.
El sueño es explosivo. Estallla. Vuelve a ser sol.

En tu castillo de diamante tu imagen se destroza y se rehace,
infatigable.

Disparo

Salta la palabra
adelante del pensamiento
adelante del sonido
la palabra salta como un caballo

The body that we sacrifice today
isn't it the God who will sacrifice tomorrow?
Imagination spurs on desire,
its kingdom is endless and as infinite as boredom,
its opposite and twin.

Death or pleasure, engulfing or vomiting,
autumn resembling the days' decline,
volcano or sex,
gust of wind, summer incinerating the crops,
stars or eye-teeth,
petrified hair of terror,
red foam of desire, massacre on the high seas,
blue rocks of delirium,
forms, images, bubbles, hunger for life,
flashes of eternity,
excesses: your measure of man.
Accept the challenge:
freedom is the choice of necessity.
Make yourself the bow and the arrow, the vocal cord and the cry.
Dream is explosive. Burst into flame. Become a sun again.

In your diamond castle your image shatters and renews itself,
tirelessly.

A Shot

The word leaps
ahead of thought
ahead of sound
the word leaps like a horse

delante del viento
como un novillo de azufre
adelante de la noche
se pierde por las calles de me cráneo
en todas partes las huellas de la fiera
en la cara del árbol el tatuaje escarlata
en la frente del torreón el tatuaje de hielo
en el sexo de la iglelsia el tatuaje eléctrico
sus uñas en tu cuello
sus patas en tu vientre
la señal violeta
el tornasol que gira hasta el blanco
hasta el grito hasta el basta
el girasol que gira como un ay desollado
la firma del sin nombre a lo largo de tu piel
en todas partes el grito que ciega
la oleada negra que cubre el pensamiento
la campana furiosa que tañe en mi frente
la campana de sangre en mi pecho
la imagen que ríe en lo alto de la torre
la palabra que revienta las palabras
la imagen que incendia todos los puentes
la desaparecida en mitad del abrazo
la vagabunda que asesina a los niños
la idiota la mentirosa la incestuosa
la corza perseguida
la mendiga profética
la muchacha que en mitad de la vida
me dispierta y me dice *acuérdate*

ahead of the wind
like a sulfur bull
ahead of the night
it loses its way in the steets of my skull
the beast's footprints are everywhere
the scarlet tattoo on the tree's face
the ice tattoo on the tower's forehead
the electric tattoo on the church's sex
its claws in your neck
its paws on your stomach
the violet sign
the sunflower turning toward the white
toward the scream toward enough
the sunflower turning like a flayed cry
the nameless signature across your skin
everywhere the blinding scream
the black wave that covers thought
the furious bell ringing in my head the bloody bell in my
 breast
the laughing image at the tower's top
the word that bursts the other words
the image that incinerates all the bridges
the woman who disappeared in the midst of an embrace
the vagabond who killed the children
the idiot the liar the incestuous woman
the doe running for her life
the prophetic beggarwoman
the girl who in the midst of life
awakens me and says *remember*

Agua Nocturna

La noche de ojos de caballo que tiemblan en la noche,
la noche de ojos de agua en el campo dormido,
está en tus ojos de caballo que tiembla,
está en tus ojos de agua secreta.

Ojos de agua de sombra,
ojos de agua de pozo,
ojos de agua de sueño.

El silencio y la soledad,
como dos pequeños animales a quienes guía la luna,
beben en esos ojos,
beben en esas aguas.

Si abres los ojos,
se abre la noche de puertas de musgo,
se abre el reino secreto del agua
que mana del centro de la noche.

Y si los cierras,
un río, una corriente dulce y silenciosa,
te inunda por dentro, avanza, te hace obscura:
la noche moja riberas en tu alma.

Nocturnal Water

Night with horse's eyes trembling in the night,
night with water eyes sleeping in the field,
is in your trembling horse eyes,
is in your eyes of secret water.

Eyes of shady water,
eyes of well water,
eyes of dream water.

Silence and solitude
like two small animals following the moon,
drink from these eyes,
drink from these waters.

If you open your eyes,
night opens its mossy doors,
water opens its secret kingdom
flowing from the center of night.

And if you close them,
a river wells up from within,
advancing, darkening you:
night dampens the shores of your soul.

Benjamin Péret

Born and raised in Rezé, near Nantes, France, Benjamin Péret (1899–1959) arrived in Paris, in 1920 and contacted André Breton, whom he knew only by reputation. Entitled *Le Passager du Transtlantique* (*The Oceanliner's Passenger*), his first book of poetry appeared the following year. One of the founders of Surrealism, Péret worked tirelessly on the movement's behalf, remaining faithful to its principles for the rest of his life. Besides authoring eleven books of Surrealist poetry, he served as co-editor of *La Révolution Surréaliste* (1924–5). In the Spanish Civil War, Péret fought with the Republicans on the Aragonese front; he was imprisoned in 1940 for his beliefs, and after his release, he moved to Mexico with his wife, the Spanish Surrealist painter Remedios Varo. Returning to Paris after the end of World War II, Péret continued to play a key role in the Surrealist movement. Besides the kaleidoscopic imagery and metaphoric density that characterize his poetry, his early compositions employ metaphors borrowed from science and mathematics.

Sur La Colline …

Sur la collline qui n'était inspirée que par les lèvres peintes
les yeux blancs s'ouvrent à la lumière de la fête
et la respiration va mourir de sa belle mort
On dirait qu'une main
se pose sur l'autre versant de la colline
et que les hommes crient
c'était du ciel de Dieu que tombaient les paroles absurdes

Maintenant partons pour la maison des algues
où nous verrons les éléments couverts par leur ombre
s'avancer comme des criminels
pour détruire le passager de demain
ô mon amie ma chère peur

Nue Comme ma Maîtresse …

Nue nue comme ma maîtresse
la lumière descend le long de mes os
et les scies du temps grincent leur chanson de charbon
car le charbon chante aujourd'hui
le charbon chante comme un liquide d'amour
un liquide aux mouvements de volume
un liquide de désespoir
Ah que le charbon est beau sur les routes tournesol
tournesol et carré
si je t'aime c'est que le sol est carré
et le temps aussi
et cependant je ne ferai jamais le tour du temps

On the Hill …

On the hill that was simply inspired by painted lips
blank eyes open to the light of a celebration
and respiration will die a fine death
One would say that a hand
rests on the other slope of the hill
and that the men are shouting
The absurd words fell from God's heaven

Now let us depart for the house of seaweed
where we will see the elements covered by their shadows
advance like criminals
to destroy tomorrow's passenger
oh my dear my dear fright

Naked as my Mistress …

Naked naked as my mistress
the light descends along my bones
and time's saws grind their charcoal songs
for the charcoal is singing today
the charcoal sings like liquid love
a liquid with voluminous movements
a liquid of despair
Ah how lovely the charcoal looks on the sunflower roads
sunflower and square
if I love you it's because the ground is square
and also time
and yet I can never encircle time

car le temps tourne comme à la roulette
la boule qui regarde
dans la mosaïque des forêts

Cerveaux et miroirs roulez
Car le charbon a la tête d'un dieu
et les dieux ô cerises les dieux aujourd'hui plantent des
 épingles
dans le cou des zouaves
et les zouaves n'ont plus de moustaches
parce qu'elles accompangent les jets d'eau
dans la course de l'avoine
l'avoine cirée lancée le long des vents à la poursuite des
 marées
Marées de mes erreurs où mîtes-vous nos vents
car vos vents sont aussi des marées
ô mon amie
vous qui êtes ma marée mon flux et mon reflux
vous qui descendez et montez comme le dégel
vous qui n'avez de sortie que dans la chute des feuilles
et ne songez point à vous échapper
car s'échapper c'est bon pour une flèche
et les flèches qui s'échappent ont frôlé tous les soupirs
mais vous qui êtes dans l'eau comme un remous
belle comme un trou dans une vitre
belle comme la rencontre imprévue d'une cataracte et d'une
 bouteille

La cataracte vous regarde belle de bouteille
la cataracte gronde parce que vous êtes belle
bouteille
parce que vous lui souriez et qu'elle regrette d'être cataracte

for time revolves like the ball
of a roulette wheel gazing
at the forests' mosaic

Roll brains and mirrors
For the charcoal has a god's head
and the gods oh cherries the gods today stick pins
in the colonial soldiers' necks
and the colonial soldiers have no mustaches
because they are accompanying the fountains
in the oat race
the waxed oats flung into the wind in pursuit of the tides
Tides of my errors where have you put our winds
for your winds are also tides
oh my friend
you who are my tide my ebb and flow
you who descend and ascend like a thaw
you whose only exit is falling leaves
and don't think of escaping
for escaping is fine for an arrow
and the arrows that escape graze all the sighs
but you who are in the water like an eddy
beautiful as a hole in a window
beautiful as the sudden encounter of a waterfall and a bottle

The waterfall is looking at you lovely bottle
the waterfall is grumbling because you are beautiful
bottle
because you are smiling at it and it regrets being a waterfall
because the sky is poorly dressed
because of you whose nudity reflects mirrors
you whose gaze kills the sick winds

parce que le ciel est vêtu pauvrement
à cause de vous dont la nudité reflète des miroirs
vous dont le regard tue les vents malades
Mon amie ma fière et mes veines
je vous attends dans le cercle le plus caché des pierres
et malgré la lance du dramatique navire
vous serez près de moi qui ne suis qu'un point noir
Et je vous attends avec le sel des spectres
dans les reflets des eaux volages
dans les malheurs des acacias
dans le silence des fentes
précieuses entre toutes parce qu'elles vous ont souri
comme sourient les nuages aux miracles
comme sourient les liquides aux enfants
comme sourient les traits aux points

Les Jeunes Filles Torturées

Près d'une maison de soleil et de cheveux blancs
une forêt se découvre des facultés de tendresse
et un esprit sceptique

Où est le voyageur demande-t-elle

Le voyageur forêt se demande de quoi demain sera fait
Il est malade et nu
Il demande des pastilles et on lui apporte des herbes folles
Il est célèbre comme la mécanique
Il demande son chien
et c'est un assassin qui vient venger une offense
La main de l'un est sur l'épaule de l'autre

My friend my fever and my veins
I await you in the remotest circle of stones
and despite the dramatic ship's lance
you will be near me who am only a black dot
and I await you with the salt of specters
in the fickle waters' reflections
in the acacias' misfortunes
in the fissures' silence
precious above all since they have smiled at you
as clouds smile at miracles
as liquids smile at children
as lines smile at points

Tortured Girls

Near a house made of sun and white hair
a forest discovers unsuspected capacities for tenderness
and a skeptical spirit.

Where is the traveler she asks

the forest traveler wonders what tomorrow will be made of
He is sick and naked
He asks for some coughdrops and they bring him crazy herbs
He is famous like the science of mechanics
He asks for his dog
and an assassin appears bent on extracting revenge
The hand of one of them is on the other's shoulder

C'est ici qu'intervient l'angoisse une très belle femme en manteau
de vison

Est-elle nue sous son manteau
Est-elle belle sous son manteau
Est-elle voluptueuse sous son manteau
Oui oui oui et oui
Elle est tout ce que vous voudrez
elle est le plaisir tout le plaisir l'unique plaisir
celui que les enfants attendent au bord de la forêt
celui que la forêt attend auprès de la maison

Quatre à Quatre

Meurtrie par les grandes grues électriques
la patte de mouche voyage cependant dans mon oeil comme nul
explorateur
Qu'il pleuve des sardines
ou vente à en tirebouchonner le mont Blanc
elle voyage sans se laisser arrêter par la tentation des parapluies
fermés
vieux sabres de panoplies
qui ne savent plus que se moucher et éternuer
Se moucher et éternuer
en voilà une vie que n'envieraient pas les carottes à la sauce
blanche
ni l'herbe qui pousse entre les pavés bordés de dentellières
sournoises comme un oeil derrière un lorgnon
comme un signal de chemin de fer qui passe du rouge au vert
sans plus crier gare

At this point anguish intervenes a gorgeous woman wearing a
mink coat

Is she naked beneath her coat
Is she lovely beneath her coat
Is she voluptuous beneath her coat
Yes yes yes and yes
She is everything one could desire
she is pleasure all the pleasure the unique pleasure
that children await on the forest's edge
that the forest awaits near the house

Four by Four

Battered by the huge electric cranes
the fly's leg undertakes an unprecedented journey in my eye
nevertheless
While it may rain sardines
or blow hard enough to unscrew Mt. Blanc
the leg travels without being tempted to investigate the closed
umbrellas
suits of armor bearing old sabers
that can only blow their noses and sneeze
Blow their noses and sneeze
carrots in white sauce would not envy that life
nor the grass sprouting between the paving stones bordered by
crafty
lace-makers like an eye behind a pince-nez
like a railroad signal changing from red to green
without warning
or a satyr hiding in a public garden

qu'un jardin public où se cache un satyre
Mais la patte de mouche ne demande rien à personne
car les professeurs ne craignent que les escaliers branlants
où le gaz réussit parfois à tuer son ennemi le rat
à coups de pierres comme un flic chassé à courre
et les étoiles qui effraient les poissons rouges
ne sont ni à vendre ni à louer
car à vrai dire ce ne sont pas des toiles mais des tartes aux
abricots
qui ont quitté la boutique du pâtissier
et errent comme un voyageur qui a perdu son train à minuit dans
une ville déserte aux becs de gaz geignant à cause de leurs
vitres cassées
Même si le voyageur rencontre une femme nue marchant sur le
bord du trottoir
parce qu'entre les maisons et elle passe un troupeau silencieux
de crocodiles épouvantés par le feu de leurs pipes
et cherchant une église avec un large bénitier
même si le voyageur rencontre cette jeune femme
il n'évitera pas l'incendie d'un magasin de confections
d'où s'enfuiront des milliers de puces qui seront tenues pour
responsables du désastre
mais si le magasin brûle comme une lampe Pigeon
le voyageur se sentira consolé
et attendra
paisiblement
bêtement
amoureusement
courageusement
tristement
ou paresseusement

But the fly's leg doesn't ask for anything
for the professors only fear the rickety staircase
where gas occasionally manages to kill an ennemy rat
by throwing stones like a cop fleeing for his life
and the stars which frighten the goldfish
are not for sale nor for rent
for actually they are not stars but apricot tarts
that have decided to leave the bakery
and wander like a traveler who has missed the midnight train in a deserted
town where the gas lamps are whining that their glass has been shattered
Even if the traveler meets a naked woman walking along the curb to avoid a
silent band of crocodiles passing between her and the houses terrified by the
fire issuing from their pipes and searching for a church with a large holy water
font even if the traveler meets this young woman he will not avoid a candy
store's fire or thousands of panic-stricken fleas who will be judged responsible
but if the store blazes like a brand name lamp
the traveler will feel consoled
and will wait
peacefully
stupidly
lovingly
bravely
sadly
or lazily

que sa barbe pousse pour se raser
et se fera une large entaille près de l'oreille
par où sortira prudent et inquiet
un petit lézard de verre
qui ne réussira jamais à retrouver le lézard de son maître
et se perdra dans la cheminée
où l'attendent pour lui faire un mauvais parti
l'épingle à cheveux l'épingle à chapeau l'épingle de cravate l'épingle
de nourrice
et cette brute de saladier écorné
qui serre déjà les poings

Allo

Mon avion en flammes mon château inondé de vin du Rhin
mon ghetto d'iris noirs mon oreille de cristal
mon rocher dévalant la fallaise pour écraser le garde champêtre
mon escargot d'opale mon moustique d'air
mon édredon de paradisiers ma chevelure d'écume noire
mon tombeau éclaté ma pluie de sauterelles rouges
mon île volante mon raisin de turquoise
ma collision d'autos folles et prudentes ma plate-bande sauvage
mon pistil de pissenlit projeté dans mon oeil
mon oignon de tulipe dans le cerveau
ma gazelle égarée dans un cinéma des boulevards
ma cassette de soleil mon fruit de volcan
mon rire d'étang caché où vont se noyer les propheètes distraits
mon inondation de cassis mon papillon de morille
ma cascade bleue comme une lame de fond qui fait le printemps
mon revolver de corail dont la bouche m'attire comme l'oeil d'un
puits

for his beard to grow so he can shave
and will give himself a nasty cut near his ear
from which a small glass lizard
will emerge prudently and anxiously
who will never manage to find his master's lizard again
and will disappear into the chimney
where he will find
the hairpin, the hat-pin the tie-pin the safety pin
waiting to beat him up
and that chipped salad bowl bully
who is already clenching his fists

Hello

My airplane in flames my chateau flooded with Rhine wine
my black iris ghetto my crystal ear
my boulder racing down the cliff to squash the rural policemen
my opal snail my air mosquito
my bird of paradise comforter my black foam hair
my tomb burst open my rain of red grasshoppers
my flying island my turquoise grape
my collision of careful and crazy cars my savage flower bed
my dandelion pistil stuck in my eye
my tulip bulb in the brain
my gazelle lost in a boulevard movie house
my sun box my volcano fruit
my secret pond laugh where distraught prophets go to drown
themselves
my flood of currents my morel butterfly
my waterfall blue as a basic blade giving birth to spring

scintillant
glacé comme le miroir où tu contemples la fuite des oiseaux-
  mouches de ton regard
perdu dans une exposition de blanc encadrée de momies
je t'aime

Clin D'oeil

Des vols de perroquets traversent ma tête quand je te vois de profil
et le ciel de graisse se strie d'éclairs bleus
qui tracent ton nom dans tous les sens
Rosa coiffée d'un tribu nègre étagée sur un escalier
où les seins aigus des femmes regardent par les yeux des hommes
Aujourd'hui je regarde par tes cheveux
Rosa d'opale du matin
et je m'éveille par tes yeux
Rosa d'armure
et je pense par tes seins d'explosion
Rosa d'étang verdi par les grenouilles
et je dors dans ton nombril de mer Caspienne
rosa d'églantine pendant la grève générale
et je m'égare entre tes épaules de voie lactée fécondée par des
  comètes
Rosa de jasmin dans la nuit de lessive
Rosa de maison hantée
Rosa de forêt noire inondée de timbres-poste bleus et verts
Rosa de cerf-volant au-dessus d'un terrain vague où se battent
  des enfants
Rosa de fumée de cigare
Rosa d'écume de mer faite cristal
Rosa

my coral revolver whose mouth fascinates me like the eye of a
twinkling well
icy as the mirror where you contemplate the flight of your gaze's
hummingbirds
lost in an exhibition of white framed with mummies
I love you

Wink

Flocks of parrots traverse my head when I see your profile
and the greasy sky is streaked with blue flashes
tracing your name in every direction
Rosa your head covered with a Negro tribe stacked on a staircase
where the women's sharp breasts observe through the men's eyes
Today I look at you through your hair
Rosa opal of morning
and I awaken through your eyes
Rosa of armor
and I think through your explosive breasts
Rosa pond turned green by all the frogs
and I sleep in your Caspian Sea navel
Rosa wild roses during the general strike
and I lose my way between your milky way shoulders fecundated
by comets
Rosa jasmine in the detergent night
Rosa hunted house
Rosa black forest flooded with blue and green postage stamps
Rosa kite flying above a no man's land where children are
fighting
Rosa cigar smoke
Rosa sea foam transformed into crystal
Rosa

Attendre

Meurtri par les grandes plaques de temps
l'homme s'avance comme les veines du marbre qui veulent se
 ménager des yeux
dans un torrent où les truites à tête de ventilateur
traînent de lourds chariots de mousse de champagne
qui noircissent tes cheveux de château-fort
où la pariétaire n'ose pas s'aventurer
de crainte d'être dévorée
au delà de la grande plaine glaciaire où les dinosaures couvent
 encore
leurs oeufs d'où ne sortiront pas de tulipes d'hématite
mais des caravanes de hérissons au ventre bleu
de crainte d'être avalées par la fontaine d'éclairs de mer
engendrée par ton regard où volent d'impalpables papillons de nuit
vêtus de gares fermées dont je cherche la clé de signal ouvert
sans rien trouver
sinon des fers à cheval gelés
qui bondissent comme un parapluie dans une oreille
et des canards d'orties fraîches
graves comme des huîtres

Waiting

Battered by the great slabs of time
man advances like marble veins that try to spare their
eyesight
in a torrent where the electric fan-headed trout
drag heavy chariots of champagne foam
that blacken your fortress hair
where the climbing nettle does not dare to venture
for fear of being devoured
beyond the broad glacial plain where dinosaurs still brood
their eggs from which no iron oxide tulips will emerge
but caravans of hedgehogs with blue bellies
for fear of being swallowed by the fountain of sea lightning
engendered by your gaze where ephemeral moths fly
dressed in decommissioned train stations for whose overt signal
key I am searching
without finding anything
but some frozen horseshoes
leaping like an umbrella in an ear
and some fresh nettle ducks
as serious as oysters

On Sonne

Un saut de puce comme une brouette dansant sur les genoux des
pavés
Une puce qui fond dans un escalier où je vivrais avec toi
et le soleil pareil à une bouteille de vin rouge
s'est fait nègre
esclave nègre fustigé
Mais je t'aime comme le coquillage aime son sable
où quelqu'un le dénichera quand le soleil aura la forme d'un haricot
qui commencera à germer comme un caillou montrant son coeur
sous l'averse
ou d'une boîte de sardines entr'ouverte
ou d'un bateau à voiles dont le foc est déchiré
Je voudrais être la projection pulvérisée du soleil sur la parure de
lierre de tes bras
ce petit insecte qui t'a chatouillée quand je t'ai connue
Non
cet éphémère de sucre irisé ne me ressemble pas plus que le gui
au chêne
qui n'a plus qu'une couronne de branches vertes où loge un
couple de rouges-gorges
Je voudrais être
car sans toi je suis à peine l'interstice entre les pavés des
prochaines barricades
J'ai tellement tes seins dans ma poitrine
que deux cratères fumant s'y dessinent comme un renne dans
une caverne
pour te recevoir comme l'armure reçoit la femme nue
attendue du fond de sa rouille
en se liquéfiant comme les vitres d'une maison qui brûle
comme un château dans une grande cheminée
pareille à un navire en dérive
sans ancre ni gouvernail
vers une île plantée d'arbres bleus qui font songer à ton nombril
une île où je voudrais dormir avec toi

Someone is Ringing

A flea's leap like a wheelbarrow dancing on the paving stones'
knees
A flea melting in a staircase where I would like to live with you
and the sun like a bottle of red wine
has become a Negro
a thrashed Negro slave
But I love you like a seashell loves sand
where someone will discover you when the sun is shaped like a
bean
that begins to sprout like a pebble displaying its heart in the
rain
or shaped like a half-opened can of sardines
or shaped like a sailing ship with a torn jib
I would like to be the sun's pulverized projection on your arms'
ivy ornaments
this tiny insect that tickled you when I met you
No
this iridescent sugar mayfly doesn't resemble me any more than
mistletoe resembles an oak
that has only a crown of green branches where a couple of robins
live
I would like to be
for without you I am no more than a crack between the next
barricades' paving stones
Your breasts press so hard against my chest
that they make two smoking craters like a reindeer in a cave
which fit you like a suit of armor fits a nude woman
awaited in the depth of its rust
by liquifying itself like the windows of a burning house
like a chateau in a great chimney
like a ship
with no anchor or rudder
drifting toward an island with blue trees evoking your navel
an island where I would like to sleep with you

Philippe Soupault

Philippe Soupault (1897–1990) was born in Chaville, France. Introduced to André Breton by Guillaume Apollinaire, he participated in the Dada movement before helping to co-found Surrealism. Soupault published his first book of poetry, *Aquarium*, in 1917. Together with Breton and Louis Aragon, he founded the journal *Littérature* in 1919. In that same year, he and Breton also authored the first Surrealist text: *Les Champs magnétiques* (*Magnetic Fields*). A second book of poetry, *Rose des Vents* (*Compass Cards*), appeared in 1920. Although Soupault collaborated on the first issues of *La Revolution Surréaliste* in 1924, he eventually ceased to participate in Surrealist activities. From 1938 to 1940, he was director of Radio Tunis, until the Vichy government imprisoned him for broadcasting a series of anti-fascist programs. Charged with UNESCO missions after the war, he traveled all over the globe.

Le Nageur

Mille cris oiseaux
l'horizon trace une ligne de vie
Et les vagues visages perdus chuchotent
dans les golfes tendus comme des bras ouverts
Je suis sûr enfin d'être seul
est-ce le Nord est-ce l'Ouest
le soleil bourdonnant de lumière
rue du ciel et de la terre
je m'arrête pour savoir encore si l'été est rouge
dans mes veines
et mon ombre tourne autour de moi
dans le sense des aiguilles d'une montre
Le sommeil m'apporte les insectes et les reptiles
la douleur une grimace et le mensonge
le réveil
je flotte visage perdu au milieu d'une heure
sans secours sans appel
je descends sans conviction des marches sans but
et je continue sans regret jusqu'au sommeil
dans les yeux des miroirs et dans le rire du vent
je reconnais un inconnu qui est moi
je ne bouge plus
j'attends
et je ferme les yeux comme un verrou
Nous ne saurons jamais quand la nuit commence
et où elle finit
mais cela en somme n'a pas beaucoup d'importance
les nègres du Kamchatka
s'endormiront ce soir près de moi
lorsque la fatigue se posera sur ma tête
comme une couronne

The Swimmer

A thousand cries birds
the horizon traces a lifeline
And the waves whisper lost faces
in the gulfs extended like open arms
I am finally certain of being alone
is it North is it West
the sun buzzing with light
celestial and terrestrial street
I stop to find out if the summer is red
in my veins
and my shadow revolves about me
clockwise
Sleep brings me insects and reptiles
pain a grimace and a lie
awakening
I float faceless in the midst of an hour
helpless with no aid in sight
without conviction I descend endless stairs
and I continue with no regret until sleep
in the mirrors' eyes and in the wind's laughter
I recognize a stranger who is me
I don't move
I wait
and I shut my eyes like a bolt
We will never know when night begins
and where it ends
but basically that doesn't much matter
the Negroes of the Kamchatka peninsula
will fall asleep tonight near me
when fatigue settles on my head
like a crown

Médaille D'or

La nuit bouscule ses étoiles
Il pleut du sable et du coton
Il fait si chaud
mais le silence tisse des soupirs
et la gloire de l'été
On signale un peu partout
des crimes de chaleur
des orages d'hommes qui vont renverser les trônes
et une grande lumière
à l'ouest
et à l'est
tendre comme l'arc-en-ciel
Il est midi
Toutes les cloches
répondent
midi
Une attente sourde
comme un grand animal
Sort ses membres de tous les coins
il avance ses piquants
ce sont les ombres et les rayons
Le ciel nous tombera sur la tête
On attend le vent
Qui aujourd'hui doit être bleu
comme un drapeau

Gold Medal

Night jostles its stars
It is raining sand and cotton
It is so hot
but the silence is weaving sighs together
and the summer's glory
Crimes of heat
manifest themselves all over
human storms destined to upset thrones
and a great light
in the West
and in the East
tender as a rainbow
It is noon
All the bells
respond
noon
Like a large animal
a muffled anticipation
stretches its limbs in every corner
it raises its spines
these are the shadows and the rays of light
The sky will fall on our heads
We await the wind
Which should be blue today
like a flag

Fleuve

Couloir longitudinal des grands bâtiments souterrains
tendance obscure des lions parasites
ô lune affreuse qui court comme une grande lueur
fleuve
les sillages des bateaux sont tes cheveux
la nuit est ton manteau
les reflets qui dorment sur toi sont tes écailles
personne ne veut plus te connaître
tu coules des yeux de cette étoile inconnue
pleurs fertilisants
mais jamais nous ne connaîtrons ta source pâle
ton adorable bouche
et ton vagissement prolongé dans les champs de ta naissance
A chaque arbre qui se penche vers toi tu dis
Passe mon ami mon frère et regarde devant toi
les espoirs sont moisis
Il n'y a plus que ce Dieu magnifique
miséricorde
et ces grands appels là-bas très près de mon coeur
cours si tu peux jusqu'à lui
Mais ne sais-tu pas que la nuit t'étranglerait
avec ses mains sanglantes
Adieu mon frère mon ami sourd
je ne sais plus si ce fleuve qui est ton frère te reverra
jamais
fleuve sinueux comme des lèvres
et comme le serpent qui dort dans ce gazon savoureux
brebis maternelle
troupeau de lueurs

River

Longitudinal corridor of great subterranean buildings
obscure tendency of parasitic lions
oh terrible moon running like a great flash
river
the boats' wakes are your hair
the night is your coat
the reflections dozing on your surface are your scales
no one wants to acknowledge you any more
you flow from that unknown star's eyes
fertilizing tears
but we will never know your pale source
your adorable mouth
and your interminable wailing in the fields of your birth
To every tree leaning toward you you say
Continue my friend my brother and look before you
hopes are moldy
Only that magnificent God remains
mercy
and those grand appeals there so close to my heart
run if you can to him
But don't you know night would strangle you
with her bloody hands
Goodbye my brother my deaf friend
I do not know if you will see your brother river again
ever
Sinuous river like human lips
and like the snake asleep in the savory grass
maternal sheep
glimmering flock

Georgia

Je ne dors pas Georgia
je lance des flèches dans la nuit Georgia
j'attends Georgia
je pense Georgia
Le feu est comme la neige Georgia
La nuit est ma voisine Georgia
j'écoute les bruits tous sans exception Georgia
je vois la fumée qui monte et qui fuit Georgia
je marche à pas de loups dans l'ombre Georgia
je cours voici la rue les faubourgs Georgia
Voici une ville qui est la même
et que je connais pas Georgia
je me hâte voici le vent Georgia
et le froid silence et la peur Georgia
je fuis Georgia
je cours Georgia
les nuages sont bas ils vont tomber Georgia
j'étends les bras Georgia
je ne ferme pas les yeux Georgia
j'appelle Georgia
je crie Georgia
j'appelle Georgia
je t'appelle Georgia
Est-ce que tu viendras Georgia
bientôt Georgia
Georgia Georgia Georgia
Georgia
je ne dors pas Georgia
je t'attends Georgia

Georgia

I can't sleep Georgia
I shoot arrows into the night Georgia
I am waiting for Georgia
I am thinking Georgia
The fire is like snow Georgia
The night is my neighbor Georgia
I listen to all the noises without exception Georgia
I see the smoke that rises and flees Georgia
I walk stealthily in the shadow Georgia
I am running here is a suburban street Georgia
Here is a town that is the same
and is unfamiliar Georgia
I am hastening here is the wind Georgia
and cold silence and fear Georgia
I am fleeing Georgia
I am running Georgia
the clouds are over there they are about to fall Georgia
I stretch out my arms Georgia
I do not close my eyes Georgia
I am calling Georgia
I am crying Georgia
I am calling Georgia
I am calling you Georgia
Will you come Georgia
soon Georgia
Georgia Georgia Georgia
Georgia
I can't sleep Georgia
I am waiting for you Georgia

Une Minute De Silence

J'abandonne ce repos trop fort
et je cours haletant vers le bourdonnement des mouches
La prophétie des mauvais jours et des soirs maigres
aboutit toujours à ce grand carrefour
celle des secondes prolongées
bondé de nuages ou de cris
On joue de grands airs
et c'est la nuit qui s'approche
avec ses faux bijoux d'étoiles
Est-ce le moment de fermer les yeux
C'est l'heure des sonneries
le grand va-et-vient des visages
et des ampoules électriques
Je n'ai pas besoin d'être seul
pour croire à la volonté à la franchise au courage
Il suffit d'un parfum couleur de tabac
ou d'un geste lourd comme une grappe

L'odeur des assassinats rôde nécessairement
Mais il y a le soir qui attend bleu comme un oiseau
Mais il y a la nuit qui est à la portée de mes mains
Mais il y a une fenêtre qui s'éclaire d'un seul coup
il y a un cri
un regard qu'on devine
un regard qui est chaud comme un animal
et ces longs appels des arbres immobiles
tout ce qui s'endort pour l'immobilité
dans la concession perpétuelle du vrai silence
et ce silence plus sincère encore d'un sommet d'ombre
que les nuages baisent d'un seul coup

A Minute of Silence

I abandon this overwhelming repose
and breathless I run toward the flies' buzzing
The prophecy of unlucky days and hungry nights
always leads to this great crossroad
the prophecy of interminable seconds
crammed with clouds or with cries
Someone is playing grand melodies
and night approaches
with her false jewelry of stars
Is it time to close my eyes
It is the hour of ringing bells
the great coming and going of faces
and of electric lightbulbs
I don't need to be alone
to believe in willpower sincerity courage
A tobacco-colored perfume suffices
or a heavy gesture like a cluster of grapes

The odor of murders prowls about inevitably
But there is evening waiting blue as a bird
But there is night within my hands' reach
But there is a window suddenly filled with light
there is a cry
a glance warm as an animal
and long appeals by the motionless trees
everything that slumbers in immobility
in the perpetual concession of true silence
and the sincerer silence yet of a shadow's summit
suddenly kissed by the clouds

Est-ce Le Vent? (Excerpt)

Est-ce le vent qui m'apporte tout à coup ces nouvelles
Là-bas des signaux des cris
et puis rien
la nuit
c'est le vent qui secoue et qui chante
Il traîne derrrière lui tout un fracas et une lente poussière
quelque chose de mou
quelque choc qui est la paresse
une de ces méduses mortes qui pourrissent
en crachant une odeur rose
c'est le vent qui pousse ces pauvres bateaux bleus
et leur fumée morose
qui secoue ces arbres malheureux
et c'est lui encore qui enivre les nuages
il rase l'herbe
Je sais que c'est lui qui pousse jusqu'à moi
cette morne lumière et ces ombres sanglantes
c'est lui toujours qui fait encore une fois battre mon coeur
Ainsi ce coup de poing que j'entends et qui frappe une poitrine nue
cette galopade de chevaux ivres d'air
Il découve le chemin qui mène là-bas
dans ce pays rouge qui est une flamme
Paris que je vois en tournant la tête
il me pouse en avant
pour fuir cet incendie qu'il alimente
Je m'accroche au bord de cette terre
j'enfonce mes pieds dans le sable
ce sable qui est une dernière étape

Is it the Wind? (Excerpt)

Is it the wind that suddenly brings me this news
Down there signals cries
and then nothing
night
The wind shudders and sings
It drags an uproar behind it and slow dust
a certain softness
a certain shock or laziness
one of those rotting jellyfish
that spit out a rosy stench
the wind blows the poor blue ships
and their gloomy smoke
it shakes the miserable trees
it intoxicates the clouds
it shaves the grass
Toward me it blows
the dreary light and the bloody shadows
it makes my heart beat once again
Whence the punch I hear striking a bare chest
those galopping horses intoxicated by the air
It uncovers the road leading afar
to the red land that is all aflame
Paris that I see turning my head
it blows me forward
where I flee the blaze it is steadily feeding
I cling to the edge of that earth
I shove my feet in the sand
the sand that is the last step
before the sea appears
that softly licks me like a brave animal

avant la mer qui est là
qui me lèche doucement comme un brave animal
et qui m'emporterait comme un vieux bout de bois
Je ne lutte pas
j'attends
et lui me pousse
en soufflant toutes ses nouvelles
en me sifflant les airs qu'il a rapportés de là-bas
il s'écrie que derriere moi
une ville flambe dans le jour et dans la nuit
qu'elle chante elle aussi
comme au jugement dernier
Je jette tout mon poids sur ce sol chaud
et je guette tout ce qu'il dit
Il est plus fort
Mais lui cherche des alliés qui sont le passé et le présent
et il s'engouffre dans mes narines
il me jette dans la bouche une boule d'air
qui m'étouffe et m'écoeure
Il n'y a plus qu'à avancer
et à faire un grand pas en avant
La route est devant moi
il n'y a pas à se tromper
elle est si large qu'on n'en voit pas les limites
seulement quelques ornières qui sont les sillages des bateaux
cette route vivante qui s'approche
avec des langues et des bras
pour vous dire que cela ira tout seul
et si vite
Cette route bleue et verte
qui recule mais qui avance

and would carry me off like an old piece of wood
I do not resist
I wait
and it blows me
whispering all its news
whistling the tunes it has brought back
it shouts that behind me
a city is flaming night and day
that the city is singing too
as on the Day of Judgement
I plant all my weight on the warm ground
and I watch whatever the wind says
It is stronger
But it searches for allies
it is stronger
it searches for allies who are the past and the present
and it rushes into my nostrils
it throws a ball of air into my mouth
that suffocates and disgusts me
The only choice left is to advance
to take a big step forward
The road stretches before me
there is no mistake
it is so wide that its edges are lost from sight
just a few ruts that are ships' wakes
the living road approaches
bearing tongues and arms
to say that everything will occur alone
and so quickly
The green and blue road
retreating and advancing

qui n'a pas de cesse et qui bondit
Et lui toujours qui siffle une chanson de route
et qui frappe dans le dos
et qui aveugle pour que l'on n'ait pas peur
Moi je m'accroche au sable qui fuit entre mes doigts
pour écouter une dernière fois encore
ce tremblement et ces cris
qui firent remuer mes bras et mes jambes
et dont le souvenir est si fort
que je veux l'écouter encore
que je voudrais le toucher
Et lui ne m'apporte qu'un peu de ce souffle
un peu de la respiration du grand animal
bien aimé

never resting but bounding forward
and still the wind whistles a traveling song
strikes one's back
blinds one to turn back fear
Myself I cling to the sand fleeing between my fingers
listening one last time
to the trembling and the cries
that caused my arms and my legs to stir
whose memory is so potent
I want to hear it again
I would like to touch it
It only conveys a trace of that breath
a trace of that great beloved animal's
breath

Selected Bibliography

Adamowicz, Elza. *Surrealist Collage in Text and Image: Dissecting the Exquisite Corpse*. Cambridge: Cambridge University Press, 1998.

Alexandrian, Sarane. *Surrealist Art*. London: Thames and Hudson, 1970.

Balakian, Anna. *Literary Origins of Surrealism: A New Mysticism in French Poetry*. New York: New York University Press, 1947.

Balakian, Anna. *Surrealism: The Road to the Absolute*. Rev. ed. Chicago: University of Chicago Press, 1986.

Bohn, Willard. *Marvelous Encounters: Surrealist Responses to Film, Art, Poetry, and Architecture*. Lewisburg, Pennsylvania: Bucknell University Press, 2005.

Bohn, Willard. *The Rise of Surrealism: Cubism, Dada, and the Pursuit of the Marvelous*. Albany: State University of New York Press, 2002.

Breton, André. *Manifestoes of Surrealism*. Tr. Richard Seaver and Helen R. Lane. Ann Arbor: University of Michigan Press, 1969.

Caws, Mary Ann. *The Poetry of Dada and Surrealism*. Princeton: Princeton University Press, 1970.

Caws, Mary Ann. *Surrealism (Themes and Movements)*, Phaidon, 2004.

Caws, Mary Ann, ed. *Surrealist Love Poems*. Chicago: University of Chicago Press, 2005.

Caws, Mary Ann, ed. *Surrealist Painters and Poets: An Anthology*. Cambridge, MA: MIT Press, 2001.

Chadwick, Whitney, ed. *Mirror Images: Women, Surrealism, and Self-Representation*. Cambridge, MA: MIT Press, 1998.

Chadwick, Whitney. *Myth in Surrealist Paintings, 1929-1939*. Ann Arbor: UMI Research Press, 1980.

Chadwick, Whitney. *Women Artists and the Surrealist Movement*. Boston: Little, Brown, 1985.

Conley, Katharine. *Automatic Woman: The Representation of Women in Surrealism*. Lincoln: University of Nebraska Press, 2008.

Conley, Katharine. *Surrealist Ghostliness*. Lincoln: University of Nebraska Press, 2013.

Durozoi, Gérard. *History of the Surrealist Movement*. Tr. Alison Anderson. Chicago: University of Chicago Press, 2002.

Gale, Matthew. *Dada and Surrealism*. London: Phaidon,1997.

Germain, Edward, ed. *English and American Surrealist Poetry*. Harmondsworth: Penguin, 1978.

Harris, Derek. Metal *Butterflies and Poisonous Lights: The Language of Surrealism in Lorca, Alberti, Cernuda, and Aleixandre*. Arncroach, Scotland: La Sirena, 1998.

Hopkins, David. *Dada and Surrealism: A Very Short Introduction*. Oxford: Oxford University Press, 2004.

Hubert, Renée Riese. *Surrealism and the Book*. Berkeley: University of California Press, 1988.

Ilie, Paul. *The Surrealist Mode in Spanish Literature*. Ann Arbor: University of Michigan Press, 1968.

Lippard, Lucy R., ed. *Surrealists on Art*. Englewood Cliffs, NJ: Prentice-Hall, 1970.

Marcovitz, Hal. *Surrealism*. Detroit: Lucent, 2008.

Matthews, J. H. *An Introduction to Surrealism*. University Park, PA: Pennsylvania State University Press, 1965.

Matthews, J. H. *The Imagery of Surrealism*. Syracuse: Syracuse University Press, 1977.

Matthews, J. H. *Languages of Surrealism*. Columbia, MO: University of Missouri Press, 1986.

Matthews, J. H. *Surrealist Poetry in France*. Syracuse: Syracuse University Press, 1969.

Matthews, J. H. *Toward the Poetics of Surrealism*. Syracuse: Syracuse University Press, 1976.

Morris, C. B. *Surrealism and Spain, 1920-1936*. Cambridge: Cambridge University Press, 1972.

Morris, C. Brian, ed. *The Surrealist Adventure in Spain*. Ottawa: Dovehouse, 1991.

Mundy, Jennifer, Vincent Gille, and Dawn Ades., eds. *Surrealism: Desire Unbound*. Princeton: Princeton University Press, 2001.

Nadeau, Maurice. *The History of Surrealism*. Tr. Richard Howard. New York: Macmillan, 1965.

Richardson, Michael. *Surrealism and Cinema*. Oxford: Berg, 2006.

Rothman, Roger. *Tiny Surrealism: Salvador Dalí and the Aesthetics of the Small*. Lincoln: University of Nebraska Press, 2012.

Waldberg, Patrick. *Surrealism*. London: Thames and Hudson, 1997.

Acknowledgments

I would especially like to thank The Program for Cultural Cooperation Between Spain's Ministry of Culture and United States' Universities, which awarded me a grant to translate the Spanish works in the present volume.

Grateful acknowledgment is also made to the following for permission to include works for which they hold the copyright: to Editions Corti for poems by Benjamin Péret, and from *Ralentir travaux* by René Char, André Breton, and Paul Eluard; to the Agencia Literaria Carmen Balcells for Pablo Neruda: "Arte poética" and "Cantares" from *Residencia en la tierra I (1925–1931)*, "Agua sexual," "Apogeo del apio," and "Oda a Federico García Lorca" from *Residencia en la tierra II* (1931–5) copyright Fundación Pablo Neruda, 2012; for Rafael Alberti, "Engaño," "El ángel del misterio,"and "El ángel falso" from *Sobre los ángeles* copyright Rafael Alberti, 1928, El alba del alhelí, S. L. and "Sin más remedio," "Espantapajaros," "Sermón de la sangre," "Dos niños," "Fragmentos de un deseo," and "Nocturno entre las musarañas" from *Sermones y moradas* copyright Rafael Alberti, 1929, El alba del alhelí, S. L.; for Vicente Aleixandre, "Vida" and "El silencio" from *Pasión de la tierra* (1935), "Palabras" from *Espadas como labios* (1930–1) and "Las águilas," "Las manos," and "El poeta" from *Sombra del paraíso* (1944) copyright Herederos de Vicente Aleixandre, 2012; to the herederos de J. V. Foix, who hold the copyright for "Es quan dormo que hi veig clar," "Les cases …," "La vila," "S'havia posat …," "Notes sobre la mar," and "Joan Miró," copyright herederos de J. V. Foix cesión cortesia de Quaderns Crema, S. A.; to Ana Yanguas Alvarez de Toledo for Luis Cernuda, "Nevada," "Carne de mar," "Cuerpo en pena," "Diré cómo nacisteis," "Telarañas cuelgan de la razón," "Unos cuerpos son como flores," and "Pasión por pasión" copyright Herederos de Luis Cernuda; to Editions Gallimard for Louis Aragon, "Mimosas" and "Serrure de sûreté" from *Le Mouvement perpétuel* copyright Editions Gallimard, Paris, 1926 and "Déclaration définitive," "Partie fine," "Tercets," and "Chanson à boire" from *La Grande Gaité*, copyright Editions Gallimard, Paris, 1929; Antonin Artaud, "Une Grande ferveur pensante …," "Poète noir," "Avec moi dieu-le-chien," and "Nuit" from *L'Ombilic des limbes* copyright Editions Gallimard, Paris, 1925; for André Breton, "Le Grand secour meurtrier," "Le Sphinx vertébral," "Le Marquis de Sade …," and "Tournesol" from *Clair de terre* copyright Editions Gallimard, Paris, 1966; "Le Puits enchanté" from *Poèmes* copyright Editions Gallimard, Paris, 1948; "Le bel oiseau déchiffrant l'inconnu au couple d'amoureux" and "Femme et oiseau" from *Constellations* copyright Editions Gallimard, Paris, 1961; for Aimé Césaire, "N"Ayez point pitié," "Soleil serpent," "Phrase," and "Prophétie" copyright Editions Gallimard, Paris, 1970; for René Char, "Plissement," "Afin qu'il n'y ait rien changé," "L'Epi de cristal égrène dans les herbes sa moisson transparente," "Marthe," and "Le Loriot" from *Fureur et mystère* copyright Editions Gallimard, Paris, 1951 and "Certitude" from *Dehors la nuit est gouvernée* copyright Editions Gallimard, Paris, 1983; for Paul Eluard, "L'Egalité des sexes," " Giorgio de Chirico," "L'Amoureuse," "Ne plus partager," "Boire," "Max Ernst," "Dans la brume …," "Sous la menace rouge," and "Au-hasard" from *Capitale de la douleur* copyright Editions Gallimard, Paris, 1926; "La Terre est bleue …" from *L'Amour la poésie* copyright Editions

Gallimard, Paris, 1929 and “Le Baiser” from *La Vie immédiate* copyright Editions Gallimard, Paris, 1967; for Marianne van Hirtum, “Tricide,” “Tigres charmants,” “Chanson de l’ours,” and “Dans ces chambres …” from *Les Insolites* copyright Editions Gallimard, Paris, 1956 and for Philippe Soupault, “Le Nageur,” “Médaille d’or,” “Fleuve,” “Georgia,” “Une minute de silence,” and “Est-ce le vent?” (extrait) from *Georgia, Epitaphes, Chansons* copyright Editions Gallimard, Paris, 2001.

Index of First Lines in English Translation

Index of First Lines in the Original Language